THE

APOCRYPHAL LITERATURE

A BRIEF INTRODUCTION

BY

CHARLES CUTLER TORREY

PROFESSOR OF SEMITIC LANGUAGES, EMERITUS
IN YALE UNIVERSITY

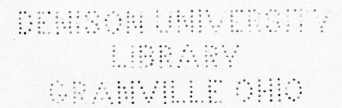
NEW HAVEN
YALE UNIVERSITY PRESS
LONDON · HUMPHREY MILFORD · OXFORD UNIVERSITY PRESS
1945

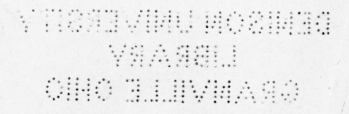

TO MY COLLEAGUES
IN THE FIELD OF SEMITIC STUDIES
IN YALE UNIVERSITY

PREFACE

A GROUP of nearly thirty documents properly classed as Old Testament literature has gained considerably in interest during the past few decades. Acquaintance with the Jewish uncanonical religious writings of the pre-Christian period is now generally recognized as belonging to the equipment of every serious student of the Bible, in either Testament, for they throw light in both directions.

There was a time when, in this country, a dozen of these "outside" scriptures known as "the Apocrypha" were as familiar in Bible-reading households as the twelve Minor Prophets; but after the controversy in Great Britain which came to a head in 1827 the English Bible ceased to contain these books, and the knowledge of them fell into neglect. The revival of interest has concerned not only the Apocrypha but also the other writings of the same character and the same early period. Many of these had long been familiar, others came to light from time to time, and all of them are now commonly included under the unsatisfactory title "Pseudepigrapha." Both groups must be taken into account in any thorough Biblical study, and cannot be ignored without serious loss.

Under these circumstances a concise handbook treating of the Jewish post-canonical literature would seem to be a real desideratum. There is at present nothing answering to this description either in this country or in Great Britain, and the present volume is an attempt to meet the need. It is indeed a brief introduction, aiming to give only the most necessary information, but it provides references which can guide the student to the most important literature in the case of any book.

A companion volume containing English translations of all the books included here would be a great convenience; but this, again, is a comparatively recent need, and is not yet provided. We have at present, for the *Apocrypha*, the English Revised Version (1896), the *Variorum Apocrypha* (Authorized Version) edited by C. J. Ball (1892), and a new translation by Edgar J. Goodspeed (1938). For the other and larger group we have the translations included in the great work (*Apocrypha and Pseudepigrapha*) edited by R. H. Charles (1913), as well as versions of single books in many scattered volumes.

It is true, indeed, that until we have texts of the apocrypha critically edited there can be no satisfactory modern translation of them. As far as the preservation of the Greek text is concerned, the apocryphal books have probably fared as well as the books of the canonical Old Testament; the scribes have shown the same faithfulness and made the same blunders in the one case as in the other. For the study of any given book it is generally not difficult to ascertain the best-preserved text, but there is always need of conjectural emendation. If the document is one of the originally Semitic group (four fifths of the whole), it will contain in addition to the usual faults of Greek transcription[1] a crop of errors of translation proportional to its extent. In the canonical scriptures, emendation of the traditional Greek is greatly assisted by the presence of the Semitic text; in the apocrypha we are without this help. The need is great of criticism from the Semitic side, by experts in Aramaic or Hebrew who know the habits of scribes and translators, and who also realize that plausible conjectures are very likely to be mistaken.

For the present we must get along with the traditional nonsense:[2] readings like the ridiculous "Manasseh," Tobit 14:10, and "Joakim the son of Zerubbabel," 1 Esd. 5:5; "torn in pieces like a bull," Sirach 6:2; "make fat thine offering as one who is not," 38:11; "Behemoth, the God of Israel," Lives of the Prophets (Daniel); After Alexander had smitten Darius, "he reigned in his stead in former time over Greece," 1 Macc. 1:1; "I will remove them the plant of uprightness," Jub. 1:16; the priests give of this gold and silver "to the harlots on the roof," Epist. Jer. 11; "If we are captured, all Judea will sit down," Judith 8:21; and the hundred other blunders that can be corrected *only* by restoring the Semitic text.

Even so, a volume of merely reprinted translations would be most welcome, while waiting for the constructive criticism that will be truly fruitful when the study of Translation-Greek shall have entered on a new era.

The present volume is intended to give account of all of the O. T. literature lying outside the canon, the books which in the usage of the early Christian Church would have been classed as "apocrypha." Two titles included here have not appeared before in the works of this description, namely, the Lives of the Prophets and the Testament of Job. The former, a collection of Palestinian legends, long familiar, has in modern times been almost lost to sight; it is commonly but erroneously regarded as a Greek compilation. The Testament of Job is an important piece of literature, only recently rescued from oblivion. It is a work of very early date, indeed it appears to be referred to, as an "Aramaic book," in the Septuagint version of Job.

One title which has appeared in all the principal recent collections of

---

1. For typical examples, reference may be made to the writer's *Second Isaiah,* pp. 213 f.
2. In each of the following examples the false rendering is explained and corrected when the present text is studied from the Semitic side.

apocryphal literature, the "Martyrdom of Isaiah," is here shown to have resulted from a mistaken conjecture; for there is no evidence of the existence, at any time, of a separate document with this or a similar title.

The dates assigned to these diversified writings are often only vaguely approximate, and the entire period covered is extensive, from the date of the second half of Baruch—perhaps the earliest of the group—to the apocalypses composed or edited in the time of the emperor Domitian. If, as sometimes happens, the dating here given to a book disagrees with conclusions which have been generally accepted, it is hoped that the reasons given for the new assignment will be carefully examined.

Recognition of the original language of each of these documents is important, especially for the eventual criticism of the existing texts. Here also new ground has been gained, and will not be lost, for by good fortune the evidence in each case is clear.[3]

The present "brief Introduction" was projected in 1894-95 in connection with a regular course of instruction in the O. T. apocryphal literature then instituted at Andover Theological Seminary. The project was never abandoned, and contributions to it were frequently made. At that time, the English R. V. of the Apocrypha had not yet appeared; Otto Zöckler's German versions of the wider group had recently been published (1891), while he remarked in his Preface that the book was *not* "meeting a long-felt want." In English, for these less-known outside books there was the able work of Edwin Cone Bissell, in the translation of Lange's Bible Commentary (1880), already out of date. Few of the students in the Seminary had ever seen an edition of the Apocrypha, to say nothing of the other books. In recent years there has been a noteworthy change, as was said at the beginning of this Preface.[4] The history of the use of these books in the Christian Church, from the beginning, is very instructive, and it is hoped that the historical sketch, the "General Introduction," will be found useful, in spite of its brevity.

New Haven, Connecticut.
December 1, 1944.

3. It must be borne in mind that the commentators and interpreters of the outside books (with the single exception to be noticed) have left the Aramaic language out of account, taking it for granted that any book of plainly Semitic origin must have been composed in Hebrew. Many detailed demonstrations of "Hebrew" underlying the Greek version can thus be supplemented and corrected with certainty when traits of Aramaic quite foreign to Hebrew are shown to be present. The one exception in the general recognition of Aramaic has been (since 1906) the section of the book of Enoch containing chaps. 18–29, in which certain Greek transliterations of Aramaic words have compelled the change of opinion.

4. There is even available, just at present, an edition of the English Bible containing the (traditional) Apocrypha, published by Thomas Nelson & Sons, New York.

CONTENTS

x   *The Apocryphal Literature*

PART I
GENERAL INTRODUCTION

OUTSIDE books" is the standing rabbinical designation of the literature which in Christian usage, ancient and modern, is commonly termed "apocryphal." All of the ancient Jewish religious writings not found in the canon of sacred scripture are included in the title, and no descriptive phrase could be more suitable. For reasons of convenience, however, it is necessary to hold also to the Christian term, which has had a long and interesting history.

The "apocrypha," in the ordinary wider use of the term, are those ancient religious writings, Jewish or Christian, which at some time were treated as divinely inspired scripture, but for one reason or another failed to gain general acceptance as canonical. Other customary use of the word will receive mention presently. The apocryphal books of the Old Testament are Jewish writings which had been abandoned by the Jews, but eventually were preserved, for the most part in Greek translation, by the Christians.

A few of these books were composed in Greek, as will be shown, but the most of them were written in Aramaic or Hebrew. The Greek translations were originally made by and for Greek-speaking Jews, and had a wide circulation also among the Gentiles. The Semitic originals all perished, and reason will be shown for believing that they were all destroyed at one time, as undesirable,[1] by official order. There are numerous cases in which not only the Semitic original but also the Greek translation has perished, and the book has been preserved in one or more secondary versions made from the Greek. Taken all together, the "outside" writings are a large group, and additions to the number are still sometimes made, as old manuscripts are discovered and deciphered. Such ancient books, for example, as the Assumption of Moses, the Testament of Job, the Book of Adam, and the Odes of Solomon were unknown (except by name) to modern scholars before the nineteenth century, but now are published.

The Christian custodians of these Jewish scriptures could not preserve them all, perhaps not always the best of them, and the story of the long process of sifting and evaluating is a most instructive chapter in the history of Christian literature. To give a brief sketch of this process is the purpose of the present General Introduction.

At the very outset, there was a preferred group of religious writings existing side by side with those of the Hebrew canon, writings familiar in every Jewish or Jewish-Christian household. These chosen few were studied and cherished, and as the Greek Old Testament took

1. "Among those who have no part in the World to Come is he who reads in the Outside Books" (Rabbi Akiba).

final shape, they formed part of it; in the earliest Christian Bibles, Greek or Latin, they were to be found. *Outside* books? By what authority? The authority was duly declared, but it continued to be disputed. Why was Esther received, and Judith excluded? What advantage for religious instruction have Ecclesiastes and the Song of Songs over the book of Wisdom and the prophecy of Baruch? If the books of Chronicles are Holy Scripture, why not also the books of Maccabees? The proverbs of Solomon are efficacious for right guidance, but so also are the proverbs of Sirach. Over these books and the few others with which they were ordinarily associated were waged the controversies which arose from time to time, down even into the nineteenth century. In a very large part of the Christian Church the most of the members of this preferred group have in the end been given the highest rank, they are *inside* books, admitted to full canonicity. Any comprehensive study of the "apocryphal" literature naturally begins with this ancient nucleus, and for present purposes the starting point may be the English Bible.

§1. The Smaller Group

In familiar English usage, "*the* Apocrypha" means the dozen books traditionally included in the English Bible but denied the rank of holy scripture. The term is equally traditional and familiar on the continent of Europe; for each of the other Protestant Bibles contained a similar collection, almost but not exactly the same. In the King James Bible of 1611 the following apocrypha are to be seen printed as a separate unit, in a sort of ghetto between the Old Testament and the New.

1. First Esdras
2. Second Esdras
3. Tobit
4. Judith
5. The Rest of the Book of Esther
6. The Wisdom of Solomon
7. The Wisdom of Jesus the son of Sirach, or Ecclesiasticus
8. Baruch with the Epistle of Jeremiah
9. The Additions to Daniel:
   The Song of the Three Holy Children
   The History of Susanna
   Bel and the Dragon
10. The Prayer of Manasses
11. First Maccabees
12. Second Maccabees

A brief preliminary sketch of the later history of this familiar and most important group will perhaps give the best approach to the wider subject.

The Wycliffe Bible (1382) contained only those books of the Old Testament which were included in the Hebrew canon. The translation was made from the Latin (of course), and the Preface accompanying it contained a paraphrase of the words of Jerome to the effect that whatever O. T. writings stood outside this canon were "without authority of belief." Jerome's word had great weight not only because he was the author of the Latin Bible but also because of his Hebrew learning. He had declared in more than one place that no Jewish book not included in the Hebrew Bible could be regarded as inspired scripture; and in his Preface to the books of Solomon he had said of such writings as Judith, Tobit, Maccabees, Sirach, and Wisdom, that they may be read for edification, but not to support Church dogmas (*ad aedificationem plebis, non ad auctoritatem ecclesiasticorum dogmatum confirmandam*). It was *authority* that Wycliffe had primarily in view in preparing his version of the Bible, and he therefore was not concerned to go beyond the "twenty-five" [2] certified books of the Hebrew canon.

Coverdale's Bible (1535) was the first in English to contain the extra-canonical books. Those which he included in the original edition were the same, with one exception, which have continued to be printed in the successive editions of the English Bible down to the present day. The exception was the Prayer of Manasseh (see below), but this was included by him in the revision of 1539, the "Great Bible." Coverdale's list seems to have been in part his own selection; it was at least not quite like any other that had been made. Any such list might indeed be called accidental, inasmuch as it included only those books which were commonly found in the Vulgate Latin manuscripts. There were good reasons, however, as will appear, why the Latin Bible had handed down these particular Jewish writings.

As regards their arrangement, a new practice was now begun. In all the existing O. T. manuscripts, whether Latin or Greek, these "outside books" were scattered about in the places where they seemed to belong, logically or chronologically; it was an innovation to put them by themselves. The first to do this was the German scholar Karlstadt, Luther's colleague and opponent, in his *Libellus de canonicis scripturis* (Wittenberg, 1520). He divided the O. T. scriptures into three classes, according to their authority. The first group comprised the books of the Hebrew canon. All the remaining books he termed "apocrypha," but

2. This is Wycliffe's own enumeration, which he justifies in his Preface. Two "official" modes of reckoning will have frequent mention in the pages of this Introduction. The one, first known in Josephus (*contra Apionem*, I, 8), counts twenty-two books (the number of the letters of the Hebrew alphabet); the other, first appearing in Second Esdras, and regular in Talmud and Midrash, reckons them as twenty-four (a favorite number). In all these systems the twelve Minor Prophets are counted as a single book.

made of them two divisions. A preferred group he termed "libri agiographi," and in this (following Jerome) he included Wisdom, Sirach, Judith, Tobit, and the two books of Maccabees. The rest, not expressly named, he pronounced worthless for Christian use.

Coverdale's second group was more liberally constituted. He translated into English *all* the books which he found in his Latin Bible; those which were outside the Hebrew canon he assembled at the end of the Old Testament and entitled THE APOCRYPHA. Martin Luther had done the same thing only one year before (1534), though his list differed from Coverdale's in that he omitted the two Esdras books and included the Prayer of Manasseh. The latter "book" made its first appearance in English in Matthew's Bible (1537) in a version made by John Rogers from the French Bible of Olivétan (1535).[3]

Luther's translation of the Apocrypha was not on a par with his other work, being made somewhat hastily from an inferior Vulgate text. Coverdale's version, which depended here very largely on Luther, was even less satisfactory. In the Geneva Bible (1560) an important innovation was made, for Whittingham and his colleagues based their translation of some of the apocryphal books on the Greek, effecting a decided improvement.[4]

In the Articles of the Church of England, as revised in 1553, Article VI (formerly V) took its stand squarely on the sole authority of the Hebrew canon, using generally the long-familiar words of Jerome. There was added a list of the O. T. books of inferior value, but this named only First and Second Esdras, Judith, Wisdom, Sirach, and two books of Maccabees. In the revision of 1571, however, the list was increased to include all the books, or parts of books, now included in the Apocrypha of the English Bible. The question of authority was in the foreground during all this time, in the Protestant churches of England and the Continent, since the doctrine of the Catholic Church, established by the Council of Trent in 1546 (see below) gave to the most of the writings of this group the rank of inspired scripture.

The translators of the King James Bible of 1611 in their version of the Apocrypha maintained the standard which was set in the Geneva Bible, not relying solely on the Latin but making use of the Greek also. In this case the Greek text employed was that of the Complutensian

3. "Olivétan" was the nickname of Pierre Robert, a cousin of Calvin. His Bible (a rather poor performance) was the first complete version in the French language. He made no independent translation of the Apocrypha, but relied entirely on the one which had been made in the Antwerp Bible of 1530. See Philippe Berger's account, in *Urtext und Uebersetzungen der Bibel* (Leipzig, 1897), pp. 191 f.

4. The "innovation" concerns merely the English Bible, for similar use of the Greek Apocrypha had been made at Geneva in 1551, in one of the French Bibles issued under Calvin's supervision.

Polyglot (1514–1517). Furthermore, this version of 1611 was not greatly altered in the revision of 1894. The English scholars in charge of the Revised Version of the Bible undertook to do for the Apocrypha what they had done for the Old and New Testaments, of course confining their efforts to that list of extra-canonical writings which had formed a part of English sacred scripture ever since Coverdale. The critical apparatus used by them was hardly adequate, and the work was not very thoroughly done; hence the revised English text of these books is still in much need of improvement.

In a general characterization of the writings of this particular group, called The Apocrypha, the most that can be said with certainty is that they are just those Jewish uncanonical scriptures which, at least from the third century onward, have been especially cherished by the Christian Church. No other writings of the same class can vie with them in this regard. Their fairly uniform presence in Vulgate manuscripts is sufficient evidence; and with the exception of Second Esdras they are to be found in every standard list of the LXX scriptures.

As to the Jewish origin, it is enough to say (taking for granted the obviously Jewish tone and interest throughout) that nearly every document in the list gives evidence of translation from a Hebrew or Aramaic original.[5] The early Christian readers were not interested in this matter, however, but adopted and used the books for their religious value. The fact that Jerome had himself translated two of their number (Tobit and Judith) and had made favorable mention of several others helped to neutralize the effect of his teaching as to the canon of inspired writings. These "Church books" (and Jerome had said of them: *legit quidem ecclesia*) naturally became sacred scripture.

§2. THE DESIGNATION "APOCRYPHA"

THE use of the term ἀπόκρυφα, as opposed to κανωνικά, to designate the writings of this or any similar group requires explanation, for there is no evident sense in which they can be regarded as "concealed" or "hid-

---

5. In the larger group also the documents originally Greek are a minority. They are the following: Second Maccabees (from 2:19), Third Maccabees, Fourth Maccabees, the Sibyllines, Wisdom (part), and the two royal letters in Esther.

Originally Hebrew: Baruch, Sirach, First Maccabees, Judith, Testaments of the Twelve Patriarchs, Psalms of Solomon, Wisdom (part), Lives of the Prophets.

Originally Aramaic: The two Letters prefixed to Second Maccabees, the Story of the Three Youths in First Esdras, Tobit, the Greek Esther, Epistle of Jeremiah, Enoch, Jubilees, Second Esdras, Apocalypse of Baruch, Assumption of Moses, Testament of Job, Apocalypse of Moses.

Also known to have existed are *secondary* Aramaic versions of Sirach (at least in part), First Maccabees, Judith, Tobit, and Testaments of the Twelve Patriarchs.

den away." In the group now under consideration there are writings prized for their religious value or their practical wisdom; historical works of importance; masterpieces of popular fiction which were given wide circulation in several languages. It is all Jewish literature of late date indeed, later than the assumed era of inspiration, but it is by no means unsuitable for public use nor to be ignored by the learned. When Karlstadt, Luther, and Coverdale employ the term, as noted above, they are merely quoting Jerome, who employs it frequently and always in the same sense: *scriptures outside the canon.* Jerome was not the author of the usage, as is sometimes assumed; for we find it in Cyril of Jerusalem, namely, in his fourth Catechetical Lecture, sections 33 and 35, where he treats the subject of Holy Scripture.

The Greek adjective, as a literary term, has a number of well-recognized meanings. It is sometimes used, most naturally, to characterize writings that are esoteric or otherwise obscure; it is thus applied, for example, to the mysterious pictures and descriptions in the Revelation of John. It is also used in a strongly disparaging sense, meaning "spurious," or "heretical"; thus in designating the apocryphal gospels, the spurious Gospel of Thomas used by the Manicheans, etc. As employed by Cyril, Jerome, and their fellows in speaking of religious books which are not canonical, it is a definitely ecclesiastical term with a recognized meaning of its own, quite distinct from either of those just given or from any other pagan use of the word. It denotes a classification, most commonly the simple notion, "outside the canon"; and it has generally been taken for granted, with good reason, that it is a Jewish or Jewish-Christian term, and that its origin must be sought in some Jewish literary usage. There is nothing to indicate, however, that the Greek word is a translation from Hebrew or Aramaic.

The theory, often proposed, of a connection with the Hebrew verb *gānaz* ("save up, treasure up") is erroneous. The verb does not mean "conceal," nor does it appear to have been used in the way supposed. The regular rabbinical designation of the extra-canonical writings is *sefārīm ḥīsōnīm*, "outside books," an admirably simple descriptive term which meets all requirements.[6] Both this term and Jerome's "apocrypha," be it noted, are widely inclusive, never confined to any definite group.

The reason why the "outside" books came to be termed "hidden" is probably to be found in certain oft-quoted passages in the Apocalypse of Ezra (variously called Second Esdras, Fourth Ezra, etc.). Chapters 12 and 14 tell how Israel's religious literature, which had been destroyed, was miraculously restored by Ezra. This literature con-

6. See A. Geiger, *Urschrift,* pp. 200 ff.

sisted of the "twenty-four" canonical books and "seventy" others; the former to be of prime authority for all Israel, while the use of the others was to be determined by the wise, through testing.

Ezra has been expressly told, more than once, that not all of Israel's divinely given books are to be handed over to the public; some are withheld, as has always been the case. He hears the voice of the Most High saying (14:6): "I brought [Moses] up to Mount Sinai, . . . and told him many wondrous things, and showed him the secrets of the times, . . . and commanded him, saying, These words shalt thou publish openly, and those shalt thou *hide*."

Likewise Ezra had been instructed in regard to his own visions (12:37 f.): "Write all these things that thou hast seen in a book, and *put them in a secret place;* and thou shalt teach them to the wise of thy people, whose hearts thou knowest are able to comprehend and keep these secrets." So now that the command is to be given regarding the restored Hebrew-Aramaic literature, just dictated to him, from the Pentateuch down to his own apocalypse, he hears the Voice saying (14:45 ff.): "The first that thou hast written [i.e., the canonical literature] publish openly, and let the worthy and the unworthy read it; but keep the seventy last, that thou mayest deliver them to such as be wise among thy people; for in them is the spring of understanding, the fountain of wisdom, and the stream of knowledge."

Here, evidently, is the origin of the ecclesiastical term, "apocrypha." The seventy books are divinely dictated, like the others, but are "hidden." This means that edifying literature, as a class, was recognized and given high value; while the fundamental superiority, the universal quality, of the twenty-four books was sharply set forth. The round number "seventy" could be stretched or diminished; and since no books were specifically named or characterized, the question of relative authority among them could not be troublesome.

Second Esdras, composed in Aramaic,[7] was written in the latter part of the first century A.D., presumably in Jerusalem. Like several other writings of the same period (see below), it might be either Jewish or Jewish-Christian in its origin. Its testimony to the existence, at that time, of a very considerable body of extra-canonical religious literature—all of it, no doubt, written in either Aramaic or Hebrew —is highly important. The account of the fate which overtook this Semitic literature is also the story of a significant turning-point in Jewish history. This matter will be touched upon in the next section.

7. See the *Jour. Bib. Lit., 61* (1942), 72–74, for sufficient evidence of this fact.

§3. The Other "Outside Books"; and a Proposed Return to the Older Use of the Term "Apocrypha"

In early Christian usage, from the 4th century onward, there were several ways of dividing the "outside books" into two classes, distinguishing a preferred few from the many which were less familiar. Those which were included in the Bible of this or that community, and therefore were accustomed to be read in church, were felt to deserve a title of their own. Even though not strictly canonical, they were at least not "hidden," and therefore they were often termed the "sacred books" (hagiographa), or the "doubtful" books (antilegomena). The term "apocrypha" was then applied especially to the remainder of this extra-canonical literature, though still used also for the whole.

The scholars of the Reformation, applying Jerome's term "apocrypha" to the little collection of uncanonical books which they took over from the Vulgate, had no special name for the other and much larger body which lay outside. This contained a number of books attributed to Adam, Enoch, Moses, and still other great men of the Bible; so conspicuous a group of writings that it soon led to the designation of the entire body as "pseudepigrapha." Thus the collections of extra-canonical Jewish literature made in the 17th century by the German scholar J. A. Fabricius include not only a complete edition of our Apocrypha (*Libri V.T. apocryphi omnes graece*, Frankfort, 1694), but also two volumes bearing the title *Codex pseudepigraphus V.T.*; final edition, Hamburg, 1722. It accordingly became customary to employ the phrase "Apocrypha and Pseudepigrapha" as a term including all this literature.

It is not a good classification. The question of pseudo-naming played no part in the selection of our Apocrypha by the Church, and the little collection has its own false attributions to Ezra, Solomon, Baruch, Jeremiah, and Manasseh. On the other hand, the majority of the so-called Pseudepigrapha are not really such, and a few of them have some historic right to be included in the Apocrypha—so far as this term can be said to have a definite meaning for the Church of the present day. A new terminology is needed. It might, indeed, seem desirable to retain, for a limited group, the time-honored name so generally applied to the best-known writings of this class; but "Apocrypha" in modern usage has not meant just the same thing everywhere, and there is so standard to which appeal could be made.

As far as English usage is concerned, a recent innovation is significant, in its abandonment of the old tradition. The great English corpus of the Jewish "outside books," *The Apocrypha and Pseudepigrapha of the Old Testament* (two vols., Oxford, 1913), prepared by many noted scholars under the editorial direction of R. H. Charles, breaks through the traditional bounds of the former group, changing what had stood unchanged for nearly four hundred years. A new member, Third Maccabees, is added to the group, while Second Esdras, which had always been a member of it, is transferred to the second volume. It would seem that the long-familiar term "Apocrypha" in its traditional sense must now go out of use, for it is not easy to see why any new edition should ever be issued of the particular documents which have stood together from the time of Coverdale to that of the Revised Version.

As for the designation "Pseudepigrapha," it has already been declared undesirable for this large and important collection of writings; first, because it does not apply to more than a part of them, and secondly, because even in the cases where the term would be in place it emphasizes unduly—and with a somewhat unpleasant sound—a feature which is of minor importance; one, moreover, which appears very conspicuously in the other group! In short, the current classification of the Jewish post-canonical literature as Apocrypha and Pseudepigrapha is outworn and misleading, supported neither by history nor by present fact; there is need of something better. I would suggest a return to the usage of St. Jerome and the early Christian Church, and to the classification of sacred literature exemplified in the Ezra apocalypse, making the term "apocrypha" include *all* the extracanonical writings. This corresponds to the convenient rabbinical designation of the Hebrew or Aramaic religious writings not included in the Canon as the "outside books."

In this volume, accordingly, the term "pseudepigrapha" will be discarded.

In the wider collection of apocryphal books we find all the characteristic forms of literature; popular narrative, edifying history, religious philosophy in various dress, poetry both didactic and lyric, proverbial wisdom, and remarkable specimens of that product of unbridled imagination called the "apocalypse." These dozens of Jewish books of which we have some knowledge are unquestionably a small survival from an extensive literature which was both religious and popular. With few exceptions they are Palestinian in origin, which (as already remarked) means in each case that the original language was Semitic. It is generally not difficult to see why these particular writings survived. Literary quality, religious content, popular appeal, attribution to one or another of the great names of Hebrew history; these and other fairly obvious considerations sufficed to keep this portion of a normally vanishing literature alive and in use.)

To what extent a few of these writings may have been treated by Jewish readers as on a par with their holy scriptures, is a difficult question, and of no great importance. The proverbs of Sirach were sometimes thus honored; but their origin was known, and they came too late for canonicity, after "the time when no prophet appeared" (1 Macc. 9:27). The most of the books were obviously of late date, or else were ruled out by other considerations. The book of Wisdom ("Wisdom of Solomon"), a noble work, was very evidently Greek in its second half. Tobit and Judith, each given an ancient setting, were plainly popular tales; moreover, Judith, in the opening sentences, expressly disclaims historical verity (in the days when "Nebuchadnezzar reigned over the Assyrians in Nineveh," etc.). The second half of Baruch (3:9–5:9) is worthy to be classed as Hebrew prophecy, and is well fitted for public reading in church or synagogue. But the book is clearly composite, of uneven literary quality, and, in its prose narrative, incongruous with accepted facts of Jewish history. The apocalypses, including Enoch, were recognized by the learned as parenetic compositions of the post-prophetic time. They made interesting reading, but there was probably no question of ranking any of them as canonical.

Such edifying books as these continued to be composed in considerable number by Palestinian Jews, and to be read by the people, until near the end of the 1st century A.D.; that is, down to the time when the overwhelming catastrophe which fell upon the nation, joined to other factors, decided its leaders to hold to the sacred books only, discarding and destroying all others (see below). In this century were produced such writings of our group as the Apocalypse of Moses (the Adam and Eve books), the Testaments of the Twelve Patriarchs, the fine Apocalypse of Ezra (Second Esdras), and the very similar Apocalypse of Baruch; these doubtless but a few out of many productions of this one century.

The Jews of the Dispersion, especially those of Egypt, contributed their minor portion to the apocryphal literature which eventually was preserved, chiefly through the medium of the Church. These books, written in Greek, were generally different in character from those which were produced in Palestine. The latter, in Greek translation, were widely popular, and a large and constant supply; how extensive the native Jewish-Greek contribution was, we have not the means of knowing. A fine example is the book known to us as Fourth Maccabees; an elaborate homily or diatribe in a setting of Greek philosophy. The

Second and Third books of Maccabees are equally remote from Semitic style and atmosphere. The Sibylline books, written in hexameters, may also be mentioned as especially characteristic.

The translation of the bulk of the post-canonical writings, even the latest, from Semitic into Greek, was the work of Jewish scholars, not of Christians; and it was by the Jews of Egypt, in the first instance, that this important literature, rejected in Palestine, was preserved, until the time when its adoption by the Christians caused it to be left in their hands. An interesting illustration is afforded by the book of Baruch, which was rendered into Greek, at least in part, by the translator of the second half of Jeremiah.[8] The existing evidence appears to show that by the Egyptian Jews this book was treated as a supplementary part of the book of Jeremiah, and was regularly joined to it in their Greek manuscripts.[9] It was also a result of their interest, no doubt, that the fragment now called "First Esdras" was rescued (as will be shown), the "book" which stands at the head of our traditional Apocrypha.

There is also, as might be expected, a distinct Christian element in the O. T. apocrypha, sometimes unmistakable, often difficult to demonstrate. A Jewish Christian of the earliest period, who wrote in Aramaic or Hebrew under the inspiration of his new faith, might compose a work equally enthusiastic in its orthodox Judaism and its Christian doctrine.[10] No one, indeed, of the apocryphal books has been found certainly to answer to this description; and those commentators who have recognized a considerable Christian influence have generally postulated rather an expansion or supplementing of Jewish writings; and this with good reason. In the apocalypses, in particular, a Christian editor or scribe would be strongly tempted to insert passages showing that Moses, or Isaiah, or Ezra, or some other ancient seer, had definitely predicted the Nazarene Messiah. Since, however, the belief in a divine and preëxistent Messiah was orthodox Jewish doctrine;

8. See Thackeray, in the *Jour. Theol. Studies,* 4, 261 ff., and his *Grammar of the Old Testament in Greek*, pp. 11–13; also R. R. Harwell, *The Principal Versions of Baruch* (Yale dissertation, 1915), pp. 59 ff.

9. This is expressly declared in the *Apostolical Constitutions* (middle of the 4th century), V, 20, where it is said that on the Day of Atonement the Jews in their assemblies read from Lamentations *and Baruch*. The authority of the statement has been questioned, but hardly on sufficient grounds. It is difficult to see any good reason why the assertion should have been invented; and it is supported by a variety of evidence (see Schürer, *Geschichte des jüd. Volkes*,[3] III, 342) tending to show that the Jews *of the Dispersion* continued to include Baruch with Jeremiah until the impact of Christian usage compelled them to be more strict. The question has nothing to do with the Jewish canon (which never and nowhere included Baruch), but only with a popular use of the Greek scriptures.

10. Such a work is the N. T. Apocalypse, thoroughly Jewish and thoroughly Christian, written in Aramaic in the year 68; see *Documents of the Primitive Church,* chap. 5.

since also the "Nazarene" interpretation of the Hebrew scriptures was not different from that of the Jewish authorities, there would be need of very definite allusions to the life, death, or resurrection of Jesus in order to establish Christian origin.

In fact, no *extensive* work of Christian hands has been clearly demonstrated in this literature. A portion of the Ascension of Isaiah, namely, the Vision (chaps. 6–11) which follows the account of the prophet's martyrdom, is entirely a Christian composition. In the second chapter of Second Esdras (a chapter which formed no part of the original work), verses 33–48 appear to be a Christian insertion. Some have been inclined to pronounce Enoch 37–71, the Messianic Parables, a Christian work, but on insufficient grounds. Otherwise, only occasional minor interpolations can be recognized in these books, the most important example being the conspicuous insertions in the Benjamin chapter 3, 9–11, of the Testaments of the Twelve Patriarchs.

Reference was made, above, to a most significant event in Israelite history, the sudden and complete abandonment, by the Jews, of their popular literature. The decision to take this step came from Palestine, and was primarily concerned with the Palestinian literature written in Aramaic or Hebrew. The last centuries B.C. had witnessed a steady outpouring of books in great variety, and the process continued without interruption until the end of the 1st century A.D. Then, however, came an abrupt change. The calamity that befell the people soon had its accompaniment in the literature. The Jews of Palestine continued to write and publish in both tongues, Hebrew (the learned language) and Aramaic (the vernacular) ; but the output now was "rabbinical" literature, all of it directly concerned with the development of Judaism. No more books like the "seventy" of Second Esdras were written, nor were these any longer copied in their original language, or even preserved.

The almost total obliteration of such a body of Semitic writings, leaving hardly a trace save in translations abroad, could have taken place only under extraordinary circumstances and for very potent reasons; and these, in the main, are well known.

After the catastrophe of the year 70, the Jews turned to the Torah and the holy scriptures, to the study of the sacred law in its widest sense, with a new degree of devotion, and of set purpose. They felt so strongly that no other writings should have even the appearance of equality with those of the sacred group, or should take attention away from them, that they were ready to discard all the "outside books." The feeling of the leaders at that time is echoed in a later Palestinian writing (*Midrash Qoheleth*, 12, 12) : "Whosoever brings together in his house more than twenty-four books (the canonical scriptures) brings confusion."

Another powerful impulse in the same direction was given by the recent appearance and circulation in Palestine of *Christian writings* in Hebrew and Aramaic, especially the latter. These had been given some toleration at first, but now became an increasing menace, and soon were fiercely opposed. The "gospel" of the Christian sect, proclaiming their Messiah, was Aramaic (Moore, *Judaism*, I, 184 f., 189), and was put forth with apologetic purpose. It was claimed by them to be inspired scripture (*ibid.*, p. 244); and this claim is attested, while rejected, in an authoritative Jewish decision of the earlier time (pp. 86 f., 243). The Revelation of John, the apocalypse of the New Testament, makes formally and repeatedly the claim to be a continuation of the Hebrew-Jewish holy scriptures (Torrey, *Documents of the Primitive Church*, pp. x f., 239–242). With a Christian Aramaic literature growing up, and the easy possibility of Christian interpolations in Jewish extra-canonical books (as shown above), the situation was intolerable; and it was chiefly this condition in the domain of literature which led to the anathema pronounced on the Christians (virtually including their books and any who should read them) by Gamaliel II, about the year 80.

Hence, as well as for the reason first given, came the determination to do away with the disturbing books, one and all, from the merely tempting to the deeply dangerous—or blasphemous. It is clear that the only effective way of doing this was to destroy, systematically and thoroughly, the Semitic originals of all the extra-canonical literature; not only the specifically Christian writings, but also all the apocrypha; and the existing evidence indicates that this was done. The saying of Rabbi Akiba, recorded in the Talmud (Jer. *Sanhedrin*, x, 1, fol. 28a; also Bab. *Sanh.*, 100b), illustrates the conviction then prevailing: Among those who *have no part in the World to Come* is "he who reads in the outside books."

The popular literature, which had had such a flourishing existence, was now discontinued as far as Palestinian Jewry was concerned. It was intended that no more books of the kind should be written, and the intention was realized. No more such works as Enoch, the Maccabean histories, Judith, the Assumption of Moses, the Psalms of Solomon, and the remaining multitude, were again composed; and in no case was the original Semitic text allowed to survive, either in Palestine or abroad;[11] a fact of the first importance for the history of the apocrypha.

11. This includes even Sirach (see § 22). But there was, and could be, no prohibition of reproducing these favorite proverbs in their original tongue, *from memory*. In fact, many of them were thus reproduced, and appear in the rabbinical literature.

Conditions in the Diaspora, meaning especially Egypt, were for a time different from those in Palestine, as will presently appear. The instruction sent out from Jamnia would concern only the Hebrew and Aramaic apocrypha that had gone abroad; there was no need to take notice of Greek translations. The latter, indeed, were eventually abandoned by the Greek-speaking Jews when the Christian Church took possession of them.

§4. The "Outside Books" in Christian Use

THE earliest literary tradition of the Christian Church was purely Jewish. It was also quite comprehensive, as has already been implied. The Jews in the last three centuries B.C. (earlier dates need not be considered here) were a literary people, prolific authors and eager readers of works dealing with their religion or their past religious history. Thus side by side with the sacred books, "Moses and the Prophets," the other class of literature distinguished in Second Esdras (see above) grew up naturally. Edifying books, prevailingly Aramaic,[12] multiplied rapidly; and, as at other times and among other peoples, a certain small proportion of these writings became especially popular and widespread in use.

When the Christians, as "the Israel of God" (Galatians 6:16), came into the inheritance—as they conceived it—of the Hebrew scriptures, they of course claimed also the popular Jewish literature with which they had been familiar from childhood. Theirs were the "seventy" books, as well as the "twenty-four." As the Gentile Christians multiplied, and the language of the Church passed over from Aramaic to Greek, at the end of the 1st century, the Christians thenceforth read the "outside books" in Greek translation. The preferred few of these writings, those which the Jews had found especially interesting and edifying, were now, in their Greek dress, read with hardly less eagerness by the Christians, who copied them often and translated them into other languages.

The writings of this class which came into more or less frequent use by the Church were by no means a definite group, as will be seen. They were the survivors out of a multitude. Many of them are known to us only by name. They were read as a supplementary division of

12. Such books as were written in Hebrew, now a learned language, were translated into Aramaic for popular use. We know this to be true of First Maccabees, Judith, and Sirach, for example. Aramaic was not only the vernacular, it was also the language of Jewish literature.

the Old Testament, certainly at first without the raising of any question of canonicity. The doctrine concerning them, judging from the way in which they are quoted, was simply this, that they were divinely given scriptures, useful for instruction, but not to be compared to the Law and the Prophets. The Jewish doctrine of holy writ, admitting to "canonicity" only such books as were believed to have been *composed in either Hebrew or Aramaic before the end of the Persian period*, was well known. There was no "Alexandrian canon," the use of the term is a mistake; the Jews had but one standard, acknowledged everywhere.

The existing evidence does indeed seem to show that the attitude of the Jews of Egypt toward the uncanonical religious books now differed from that of their brethren in the holy land. The latter, as was said in the foregoing pages, refrained on principle after the 1st century from making any use of these unnecessary scriptures. The Egyptian Jews had joined with the Palestinians in rooting out the Hebrew and Aramaic texts of books outside the sacred group; the *total* disappearance of the originals is evidence of this; they were not inclined, however, like the others, to attempt to limit religious reading to the Law, the Prophets, and the few especially favored "Writings," [13] but for some time preserved and used in Greek translation the multitude of "apocryphal" scriptures—which soon began to be taken over by the Christians.

Hebrew and Aramaic were in constant use in Jewish Egypt (as in the Diaspora generally); to the learned men, indeed, both were indispensable; but the language in common use was Greek. It is evident from the subsequent history that some extra-canonical books in their Greek dress were included, and regularly copied, in the Greek codices (see below) containing the sacred scriptures of the Egyptian Jews. These books were recognized, unquestionably, as uncanonical; the *Hebrew* scriptures were the standard in Egypt, as everywhere else; but popular custom made just such exceptions here as were made at a later day in the usage of the Church. The interesting case of the book of Baruch has already been mentioned. It must be borne in mind, that while all these scriptures, canonical and uncanonical, were held to be inspired, there were degrees of inspiration; the Prophets, for example, are not on the same plane with the Pentateuch. [14]

In Egypt, as in Palestine, the Church began in the Synagogue.

13. Even in Palestine, and for some time after the beginning of the second century, there was uncertainty as to the status of two or three books of this group.

14. E. R. Goodenough, *By Light, Light,* pp. 72 ff., has made this very clear in the case of Philo's doctrine and usage.

From the middle of the 1st century until nearly its end, the followers of Jesus the Messiah of Israel were merely a sect of the Jews. It was from the Jewish use, in Egypt, of the apocrypha that the Christians derived their own use.

§5. IN THE NEW TESTAMENT

IN the writings of the New Testament, apocrypha are occasionally quoted from, or alluded to, as would be expected. Both the writers and their Jewish-Christian readers were familiar with the considerable body of extra-Biblical scripture, and with its literary use. In so far as it was religious and edifying, it was divinely inspired (θεόπνευστος, 2 Tim. 3:16), and the manner of quoting or alluding to it is likely to be the same as in the case of canonical books. In general, the apocryphal scriptures were left unnoticed (as were also Esther, Ecclesiastes, and Song of Songs), simply because their importance to the teachings of the nascent Church was not obvious.

In the Gospels, there is a single example, the quotation from a lost book in Matt. 23: 34, 35, and Luke 11: 49–51a. In Luke, this is introduced by the words: "The *Wisdom of God* says." This appears to be the title of a book, and such it probably is, though we have no other knowledge of it.[15] The phrase is not Luke's, for he is translating, and is extremely faithful to his sources. The lack in Matthew of any formula of citation is remarkable, but the evangelist could not fail to recognize the fact of quotation.

There are in the Gospels two other passages which have often been regarded as quotations from apocryphal books. The first of these is Matt. 27:9, the prophecy concerning the thirty pieces of silver and the potter's field, quoted in the main from Zech. 11:13, but ascribed to Jeremiah. Saint Jerome tells us, in his commentary on the passage, that a member of the Nazarene sect showed him an "apocryphal" Jeremiah text in which Matthew's quotation was to be seen in its exact form (*ad verbum*); apparently an example of harmonization, by the Nazarene sect or some other, for the source of the passage was certainly the Gospel. In fact, Matthew deals with this prophecy in a characteristically rabbinic way, ascribing it to Jeremiah, whose testimony he especially needs here, apparently under the assumption that the prophet's cousin Hanamel, from whom he purchased a field for a certain number of shekels (32:9), was the potter mentioned in 18:1.

15. See the discussion of the passage, with some conjecture regarding its source, in my *Four Gospels,* pp. 277 f.

Thus the tragedy of Judas was foretold by more than one prophet. See the discussion of the passages in the chapter on the quotations in Matthew in *Documents of the Primitive Church.*

The other passage is John 7:38, where our Greek text, professedly citing sacred scripture, has the astonishing words: "Out of his belly shall flow rivers of living water." The very obvious mistranslation is explained, with ocular demonstration, in *Our Translated Gospels,* pp. 108–111. The allusion, not a direct quotation, is to Ps. 46:4 f., and the reading should be: "Out of the midst of her [Jerusalem] shall flow rivers of living water."

The most noticeable case of formal citation, by a N. T. writer, of one of the apocrypha is in the Epistle of Jude, vss. 14 f., where the words of Enoch, "the seventh from Adam," are given. The passage (probably quoted from memory, as was usually the case) is found in Enoch 1:9; cf. 5:4 and 27:2. Jude 6 also has Enoch in mind.

It happens that in this same little document there is literary allusion to another apocryphon, and verbal quotation from it. The contest of Michael and the devil over the body of Moses, mentioned in Jude 9, is a feature derived from the Assumption of Moses, as Origen tells us. We possess today only a fragment of the book, and cannot verify the quotation. See the description of the Assumption in the sequel.

Second Peter, which is so largely a duplicate of Jude, has its parallels, but with no trace of a literary allusion. Thus 2 Peter 2:4 corresponds to Jude 6, and 2:11 to Jude 8 f. It may also be remarked, in this connection, that the doctrine of the "imprisoned spirits" in 1 Peter 3:19 is derived from Enoch, chapters 14 and 15.

Another lost book to which definite allusion is made is the book of *Jannes and Jambres,* cited in 2 Tim. 3:8 in a manner that implies its familiarity to all readers. There are various references to it in the literature of the first few centuries, see Schürer, *Geschichte,* III, 292 f. The second name is also given as Mambres, thus always in the Western (Latin) texts; Mamrē in the Talmud. The *Decretum Gelasii* (c. 380) gives the interesting title, *Poenitentia J. et M.* Jannes the magician is mentioned in Pliny's *Hist. Nat.,* XXX, 1, 11, as a personage known to Jewish lore.

1 Cor. 2:9 cites as holy scripture: "Things which eye has not seen nor ear heard," etc. Origen, followed by others, says that the quotation is from an Apocalypse of Elijah, but we have no means of verifying this. Is. 64:4, which is often compared, can hardly have been the source, but may have given the suggestion to another writer.

In Eph. 5:14 there is the fine bit of Messianic prophecy, evidently well known, but from no Biblical source: "Awake, you who are sleeping, and arise from the dead, and the Messiah will shine upon you."

This is doubtless from a pre-Christian document, but we have no trustworthy information in regard to it.

There is yet another formal citation, seemingly, of an "outside book," perhaps the most perplexing case of them all, in James 4:5 f. The text here is incoherent. After "the scripture says (λέγει)," a quotation must follow; the treatment of verse 5 in the English Revised Version is not plausible. If verse 5b is such a quotation, it not only is unknown scripture, but the text is also defective, for there is no logical connection between verses 5 and 6. The word "greater" (μείζονα) is impossible in the absence of any preceding clause or sentence regarding the virtue of humility. The desperate hypothesis of a defective text has its justification here, both because of the intolerable transition and also because of other evidence that the text of this little "epistle" has had an unusual history.

Not a few scholars have been inclined to recognize in James a Christian adaptation of Jewish "wisdom" literature, whether derived from a single document or from more than one source. Justification for this conjecture is found in the extremely slight and superficial specifically Christian element in the work, contrasting it sharply with all other N. T. books. No ground for a sure conclusion, however, has been found in either the rhetorical form or the language.[16] But the book was for a considerable time held in slight regard, as we know, and consequently was neglected; hence, probably, some of the striking obscurities, and a few clearer evidences of textual corruption.[17] Some "scripture" is quoted in 4:5, but it seems likely that at the end of the verse a passage has been lost.

In addition to the cases of actual citation of apocrypha, there are in the New Testament numerous passages which at one time or another and by this or that commentator have been believed to contain *allusion to* uncanonical scripture. In a very few of these passages, the fact of such allusion is clearly evident, but in the most of them it is more or less doubtful. Examples from Jude and First and Second Peter have already been mentioned. A comprehensive collection of the supposed allusions (too comprehensive to be recommended to the ordinary student) was published by the German scholar Friedrich Bleek in the *Theol. Studien und Kritiken, 26* (1853), 268–354.

16. The language, however, is clearly translation-Greek, more or less revised.

17. The following may be mentioned. 1:12. The omission of ὁ θεός in the last clause seems very unlikely (see 2:5); it may have been omitted because of Rev. 2:10. 2:8. μέντοι is hardly suitable; and the article could *not* be omitted here (in spite of Ropes, *Comm.*). Read μὲν τόν. 4:2. Certainly φθονεύετε, not φονεύετε. 5:3. ὡς πῦρ is a Semitism; cf. Rev. 4:6; 8:8; 9:7; 15:2, etc. There must be a colon after ἔσται· then follows: "There will devour your flesh the likeness of fire, which (ὅ omitted) you have stored up in the last days" (cf. Rom. 2:5!, also Prov. 1:18 [Greek], Enoch 98:3, etc). 5:11. Read perhaps τὸ ἔλεος instead of τὸ τέλος, which is awkward.

The author of the stirring homily known as the Epistle to the Hebrews shows plainly his own acquaintance with books of the apocrypha, as many have observed. In 11:34, 35 he has in mind the narrative of 2 Macc. 6:18–7:42, as is made evident by the Greek words which he uses; compare also the last clause of verse 35 with 2 Macc. 7:9. "Sawn asunder," in verse 37, is probably an allusion to the Ascension of Isaiah, chapter 5 (see § 34), or to some earlier narrative of the prophet's martyrdom. In Heb. 1: 1–3 there are two rare Greek words which seem reminiscent of the eloquent passage in the Wisdom of Solomon, 7: 22–26: "manifold, by divers portions," and "effulgence."

In Paul's Epistles there are several passages which suggest his familiarity with this deeply religious book (Wisdom of Solomon), though the evidence is not conclusive. Rom. 1: 20–32, the passage treating of the degeneration of morals among heathen peoples, is strikingly parallel, in both matter and expression, to Wisd. 14: 22–31. Rom. 9:21, the figure of the clay and the potter, says just what is said in Wisd. 15:7, yet the parallel may be accidental. 2 Cor. 5:4, with its "tabernacle" which is "burdened," might seem to have been suggested by the very similar verse, Wisd. 9:15; but the same idea, and the same two words employed for its expression, are familiar in Greek writers from Plato downward. The "armor of God" in Eph. 6: 13–17 reminds of the same figure in Wisd. 5: 18–20. The correspondence does not extend to particulars, yet it is possible that the earlier passage suggested the figure to Paul. There is indeed good evidence that he had read the Testaments of the Twelve Patriarchs, see the passages quoted in Charles, *Pseudepigrapha*, p. 292.

The Epistle of James, a characteristic bit of "wisdom literature," has numerous points of contact with the wisdom books of the apocrypha, especially the proverbs of Sirach (Ecclesiasticus) and the Wisdom of Solomon, and the search for such parallels as would indicate literary dependence has often been made. The best collection is that in J. B. Mayor's commentary on James, third edition, chapter 4. Popular ethics and maxims, however (the mischief caused by the tongue, the uncertainty of the morrow, the folly of riches, the reward of patience, etc.), have much the same expression at different times and in different places. The conclusion reached by J. H. Ropes, *The Epistle of St. James*, p. 19, that the author of the work, while he very probably was familiar with the writings in question, does not anywhere show dependence on them, seems to be the safest.

A similar conclusion commends itself in regard to the numerous other supposed references in the New Testament to apocryphal books, especially Sirach, Wisdom, and Enoch. In no such case is there clear evidence of a literary allusion.

In general, as was said above, the N. T. writers appear to represent
the view of the apocrypha which is so clearly set forth in Second Esdras; namely, that all these writings are divinely inspired and "profit-
able for instruction in righteousness" (2 Tim. 3:16), but are not on
a par with the books of the Jewish canon.

§6. In the Early Church

During the first three centuries the leaders of the Church were not
especially concerned with the authority of the apocrypha; the question
had not assumed importance. For a long time the prime authority for
Christian doctrine was that of individuals and of oral tradition; documents, excepting always the canonical scriptures, were of secondary
importance. Eventually, along with the necessity of forming a sacred
canon of specifically Christian writings, came the need of making
some distinction among the "outside books" which the Church had
taken over from the Jews. When official lists of the new Bible began to
be compiled, it was seen that they contained books (not always the
same ones) which neither belonged to the Hebrew canon nor were of
Christian origin. Thus, in the Muratorian fragment (c. A.D. 180)
the Wisdom of Solomon happens to be mentioned as accepted. (It was
at about this time that the doctrine of N. T. scriptures of equal authority with those of the O. T. began to gain a firm hold.) Since in this
fragment the list of O. T. books is missing, we do not know what other
apocrypha may have been named.

We learn from future lists[18] that the Additions to the Hebrew
canonical books were ordinarily included even though not expressly
mentioned. It is not to be doubted that the Daniel of the earliest
Christian scriptures contained the Song of the Three Holy Children,
the history of Susanna, and Bel and the Dragon. Esther is always the
Greek book, widely different from the Hebrew. Esdras, in these catalogues of canonical books, usually means First Esdras, Ezra, and
Nehemiah. Jeremiah, in the earlier lists, included Lamentations,
Baruch, and the Epistle. This probably had been the case in the
scriptures of the Greek-speaking Jews; see what was said, above, in
regard to the book of Baruch.

In general, the books of the O. T. apocrypha which gradually
gained an especially favored place in Christian use, and eventually
came to be included among the sacred scriptures of the Church, were

18. For the successive lists of books accepted as canonical by the Church, see B. F.
Westcott's *General Survey of the History of The Canon;* Th. Zahn, *Geschichte des N. T.
Kanons,* Vol. II (1890); and E. Preuschen's very convenient *Analecta,* pp. 129–171.

those which had been similarly preferred by the Greek-speaking Jews. The first factor in their favor, accordingly, was Jewish tradition based on the evident importance of the books themselves, either as supplementing the canonical scriptures or as possessing especial religious value. The second factor, perhaps equally potent in its ultimate influence, was the use of the bound book, or codex.

In the 2d century A.D. the book, or codex, was already in use to some extent for copies of the Jewish sacred scriptures, replacing the roll. This was the case not only in the Greek cities, but also in Jerusalem. We read in the Talmud (*Baba Bathra* 13b; 2d century) of codices containing the entire canonical Old Testament, and of a codex containing the Prophets only. The innovation was approved by some noted authorities, while others expressed their dissent. The book form was found more convenient, for several reasons; for use in the synagogue, however, only the roll was permitted.

For the sacred books of the Christians—both Old Testament and New Testament—the codex seems to have been preferred from the first.[19] In particular, it had the great advantage of giving quick and easy access to the scriptures of the Old Covenant, on which the Christians based themselves at all times and for every purpose. Whatever use there may have been of the papyrus roll was confined to the earliest period.

The relative stability thus given to the tradition of Christian scripture is obvious. The book, as contrasted with a collection of rolls, was a unity, with its contexts in a fixed order; and these were repeatedly copied with little or no variation, all the time becoming more and more familiar and gaining in authority. The limits of the Hebrew canon were not forgotten, but it was natural to treat as inspired scripture whatever was found between the covers of the O. T. codex. The lists of the Church's "canonical books" which from time to time were drawn up show nevertheless some divergence; a few of them, moreover, contain supplementary lists of Jewish apocrypha which testify to the wide acquaintance of the Christians with this steadily vanishing literature.

In the Codex Claromontanus[20] there is preserved a list, probably of the third century, which names among the O. T. scriptures Wisdom of Solomon, Sirach, First, Second, and Fourth Maccabees, Judith, and Tobit. (Recollect also what was said above in regard to the titles "Jeremiah," "Daniel," and "Esdras.")

Very similar to the above list, differing from it indeed only in the omission of Fourth Maccabees, is the Canon of the Synod of Carthage

19. See the valuable article by C. C. McCown, "Codex and Roll in the New Testament," *Harvard Theol. Rev.*, *34* (1941), 219–250.
20. A Graeco-Latin uncial manuscript of the 6th century, now in Paris.

(year 397). Its preamble directs that only "canonical" books are to be read in church as holy scripture; and at the end of the list there is an appeal to the authority of Church tradition: these books are named as forming a class by themselves *quia a patribus ista accepimus in ecclesia legenda.* Note that all the books which constitute our English Apocrypha are included, excepting Second Esdras and the Prayer of Manasseh.

The Synod of Laodicea (year 363), on the other hand, had aimed to hold to the Jewish canon. Its catalogue of the sacred books accordingly *omits* Wisdom of Solomon, Sirach, Tobit, Judith, and the two books of Maccabees. Observe that along with Jeremiah, Baruch and the Epistle are expressly named as canonical; while under Esdras, Esther, and Daniel the expansions belonging to the Greek tradition are necessarily included. The brief Preface recognizes the existence of other religious books (ἀκανόνιστα βιβλία), but directs that they shall not be read in church.[21]

There may also be included here, for its interest in several particulars, the famous Catalogue of the "Sixty Canonical Books" (date uncertain, but earlier than the 7th century). First comes a list of the sixty, including both Testaments. The O. T. list is that of the Jewish canon, with the omission of Esther. Baruch and the Epistle are certainly included under Jeremiah; Daniel of course contains the Additions; Esdras is presumably tripartite. After the N. T. scriptures follows a list of nine books which are described as *outside the sixty.* These are: Wisdom of Solomon, Wisdom of Sirach, four books of Maccabees, Esther, Judith, and Tobit. Last of all comes a list of "Apocrypha," of both Testaments. Those belonging to the Old Testament are the following: Adam, Enoch, Lamech, Patriarchs, Prayer of Joseph, Eldad and Modad, Testament of Moses, Assumption of Moses, Psalms of Solomon, Apocalypse of Elijah, Vision of Isaiah, and Apocalypses of Zephaniah, Zachariah, and Ezra.

The designation here of certain books (these found in the average Christian codex) as "outside the sixty," and yet not to be numbered among the "apocrypha," represents a classification which appears and reappears. In sections 1 and 3 of this volume it has been briefly mentioned how Jerome, that stickler for the Hebrew authority, was nevertheless constrained to grant a secondary rank to certain uncanonical "Church books" (some of which he translated), distinguishing them,

21. It is perhaps unnecessary to say in regard to these synods and councils that their decisions, while historically important, had only local authority. The Synod of Laodicea, for example, was a small gathering of clergy from various parts of Phrygia and Lydia. As to the origin of the lists here mentioned: the one preserved in the Codex Claromontanus probably originated in Africa; that of the "Sixty Canonical Books," in Asia Minor.

as *libri agiographi,* from the *libri apocryphi.* Others before him had done the same; notably Athanasius, when in the thirty-ninth of his Festal Letters (year 365) he presented his own catalogue of the canonical scriptures. After finishing the list he added, "for the sake of exactness," that there were certain other books, not canonical indeed, but appointed by the Fathers to be read for religious instruction; and he names Wisdom of Solomon, Sirach, Esther, Judith, and Tobit (also in the New Testament the Teaching of the Apostles and the Shepherd of Hermas).

It is unnecessary here to take account of the doctrine of individual leaders of the Church concerning the apocrypha. A few words may be said, however, in regard to the teaching of Cyril of Jerusalem (315–386), as both typical and influential. It was remarked, in a previous portion of this history, that Cyril anticipated Jerome in his use of the word "apocrypha"; and it is true that in other respects also he was Jerome's forerunner. In the fourth Catechetical Lecture, Section 35, he charges his hearer, the catechumen, to hold fast to "the twenty-two books," and *to have nothing to do with the apocrypha.* He says this in two different places, and it would be natural to conclude that he held all the books outside the Hebrew canon to be worthless for religious instruction. This is not quite the fact, however. Like Jerome, he had a profound sense of the difference between divine oracles and mere human wisdom, and he gives a counsel of perfection which could not be maintained because of Church usage.

He implies, in the passage named, that only the twenty-two books are read in church; but we can be sure that this was not the case, even in Jerusalem. The "Church books," whether given authority or not, had long been in use, everywhere. In Section 33 of this same lecture, Cyril mentions not only the universally "acknowledged" scriptures (ὁμολογούμενα), but also such as were ἀμφιβαλλόμενα. There were, then, "doubtful" books, and some freedom of ecclesiastical use. In Cyril's own list of the canonical "twenty-two" he includes under Jeremiah not only Lamentations, but also Baruch and the Epistle—these two *not* acknowledged as canonical by the Palestinian Jewish authorities. In Lecture 9, Section 2, he quotes from the book of Wisdom, and ascribes it to Solomon. In spite of the firmly intrenched and rightly accepted Palestinian doctrine, Cyril's actual practice was like that of Athanasius and Jerome.

Two powerful forces pulled in opposite directions. The Christian scholars had before their eyes the unchanging list of the Hebrew scriptures, acknowledged throughout the Israelite world; and since the Jews had been "intrusted with the oracles of God" (Rom. 3:2), the authority of their Canon was not to be lightly set aside. Opposite this, and seeming to call in question its finality, stood the Church tradition. A handful of other religious writings, taken over from the Jews themselves, and endeared to the Christians through generations of reading and study, formed part of the Church's Bible. It is true that no one of these particular writings is ever quoted in the New Testament, and the fact was noticed. However, certain other extra-canonical books *were* thus quoted, and the one fact offset the other.

The leaders of the Church in their ordinary usage doubtless treated all the sacred books, canonical and uncanonical, alike. When the question was asked, in regard to the latter, whether they were to be given equal rank with the books of the Hebrew Canon, the strictest of the scholars answered in the negative; only qualifying the refusal by admitting the rejected books "for Church reading," or else as "of disputed authority" (*antilegomena,* a designation which frequently occurs). Others, however, gave their express authority to the looser attitude. Tertullian quotes Enoch (more than once) as divinely inspired scripture. Origen does the same with First Maccabees. Cyprian cites as *scriptura divina* more than half the books of our Apocrypha.

The doctrine of the Church's authority in this matter gained ground, especially in the West. Augustine, its most famous exponent, was at first inclined to give the "Church books" equal rank with those of the Hebrew canon. In his *De Doctrina Christiana,* written in the closing years of the 4th century, he admits, indeed, that the partial rejection of a book detracts from its authority; but argues that since there is difference of opinion and no sufficient criterion of judgment, the verdict of a few great scholars (*graviores*) often outweighing the vote of the majority (*plures*), it is better to make no distinction. He accordingly accepts by name, as canonical and authoritative, Wisdom, Sirach, Tobit, Esther, Judith, First and Second Maccabees, and (apparently) First Esdras. Along with Jeremiah and Daniel he of course included the later additions.

In his latest writings, however, Augustine made concessions to the view that there should be a distinction between the books of the Hebrew canon and the "deuterocanonical" books accepted and read by the churches. His doctrine at this time differed little from that of Jerome; and both bore much resemblance to that first given expression in Second Esdras. Augustine's view had very great influence in the Church, and was paramount in the West even in the age of the Reformation.

An early forerunner of the "apocrypha controversy" is the debate which took place in the year 238 between two of the most noted Christian scholars of that day, Julius Africanus of Emmaus (Nicopolis) in Palestine and the mighty Origen of Alexandria. The latter had been heard to quote the story of Susanna as divine scripture, and the veteran Africanus, who addresses Origen as "my son," now sends him a letter of some length expressing surprise and asking for information. The story of Susanna, he says, is not extant in Hebrew nor acknowledged by the Jews. A play on words in the Greek proves that the story was composed in that language and cannot have been translated from Hebrew.[22] How, then, can it be treated as part of the prophecy of Daniel?

Origen replies in a full and elaborate letter (*Ep. ad Africanum*),[23] and is at an evident disadvantage. The Church, he holds, has an authority not derived from the Jews, and may it not be invoked in this matter of sacred scripture? It might be expected that a special Providence would guide the Christian doctrine. He appeals to prescriptive right, quoting Prov. 22:28, "Remove not the ancient landmark, which thy fathers have set." But in spite of Origen's wordy defense, the victory in the debate belongs clearly to Africanus.

The lists of apocrypha which have been presented here include as a rule merely the few preferred books. Other titles, such as those contained in the list of the "Sixty Canonical Books," the Decree of Gelasius (late 5th century), and the Stichometry of Nicephorus (9th century), give incidental evidence of a considerably larger collection of writings of Jewish origin which for a long time continued to be read and copied by the Christians. A few of these have survived in the Greek in which they were originally received, others only in secondary translations in Latin, Syriac, Ethiopic, Coptic, or Armenian. Books of mainly Jewish interest, such as the book of Jubilees, with no strong appeal for the Christians, fell early into disuse. Enoch, in spite of its attestation in the New Testament, was too bulky, and perhaps too tiresome, in comparison with its value for Christian reading, to be often copied. Some books known to us only by title were still in use in the late Middle Ages, as will be seen.

Two of the deuterocanonical books included by the principal Reformed Churches in their list had a peculiar history, unlike that of any of the other books. *Second Esdras*, otherwise known as Fourth Ezra or as the Apocalypse of Ezra, though received by the early Christians as a Greek translation, is found in no Greek manuscript, and no sure quotation from it in this language has survived. It was rendered into Latin at an early date, and is handed down in numerous Vulgate codices. Its unusual interest led to its ultimate adoption. *The Prayer of Manasseh* is found in only a few Greek Biblical manuscripts, where it occurs as one of a group of canticles appended to the Psalter. The

---

22. The argument from the word-play (in vss. 54 f. and 58 f.), long accepted as valid, is in modern times discounted.

23. One of the only two letters of Origen which have been preserved.

Latin version seems to have been made at a comparatively late day, and no Vulgate manuscript earlier than the 13th century has been found to contain it. The religious interest of the little document, added to the mention of Manasseh's prayer in 2 Chron. 33:13, 18, 19, led to its gradual inclusion in printed editions of the Bible, in spite of the clear evidence that it is historically a late intruder.

As to the arrangement of the apocryphal books in the Biblical manuscripts, it can only be said that the most of them have no secure resting place. Baruch and the Epistle were firmly attached to Jeremiah from the first; the additions to Daniel usually accompanied the prophecy; otherwise there is no regularity, but utter confusion, in either Greek or Latin codices.

It has been shown in the preceding pages that the Christians received their apocrypha from the Hellenistic Jews. In one important branch of the Church, however, this was not the case. The earliest Biblical tradition of the Syriac-speaking Church was under strong Jewish influence, and the Old Testament of the Syriac Christian Bible originally contained only the books of the Hebrew Canon (*minus* Chronicles, Ezra-Nehemiah, and Esther), with the single exception of Sirach—showing the high regard in which the book was held by the Jews. Eventually, under the powerful influence of Church usage in the Graeco-Roman world, the main branches of the Syriac-speaking Church adopted the principal "outside books," and treated them as canonical. The Nestorians, indeed, resisted the innovation, and apocryphal books are not ordinarily found in their manuscripts, nor does it appear that they (with one exception) were ever given the rank of canonical scripture.

We have testimony of unusual interest from the middle of the 6th century. Junilius Africanus, who held the office of quaestor at the court of Justinian, became acquainted at Constantinople with a scholar named Paul, who had been a professor in the famous theological school at Nisibis in Mesopotamia.[24] Paul had with him the manuscript of the course of lectures on Biblical Introduction which he had been accustomed to deliver to his first-year students. Junilius was so impressed with it that he sent a Latin translation to his friend Primasius, bishop of Adrumetum in North Africa. It was preserved and copied (under the name of Junilius) and long used as a textbook in the West, where it exercised considerable influence.

Its teaching in regard to the scriptures of the Old Testament may be summarized as follows.

The classes of literature represented are three: historical, prophetic,

24. See the article by G. F. Moore, "The Theological School at Nisibis," in *Studies in the History of Religions Presented to C. H. Toy* (New York, 1912), pp. 255-267.

and gnomic. Of the books included, some are of perfect authority, never doubted; some are of qualified authority, their title to canonicity having been called in question; others are to be rejected as uncanonical. To the first division, those of perfect authority, belong the historical books, from Genesis to Second Kings; the prophetic books, those of the Hebrew canon (and here the Psalter is included); and the gnomic books, Proverbs and Sirach.

Regarding the books of qualified authority, he says that "many" would include in the first division the two books of Chronicles, Job, Tobit, Ezra and Nehemiah, Judith, Esther, and two books of Maccabees.

The remaining books are classed by him as of *no* authority; but he adds, that "some" would include Wisdom and Song of Songs in the canonical list. Ecclesiastes is not mentioned at all.

This specimen of Biblical criticism is thoroughly characteristic of one of the most learned and liberal branches of the ancient church.

§7. In the Reformation, and After

Martin Luther and his fellow Reformers, in cutting loose from the authority of the Mother Church, were greatly concerned with the question of authoritative scripture. In this they were not alone. The old problem of drawing the line between the word of God and the outgivings of human teachers had recently been brought into the foreground in all the Western Church. In particular, the conception of divine oracles *in their true verbal form* had been gaining new importance. It was not supposed that Latin was the original language, but it had been permitted to hold the field. At the time (1513) when Cardinal Ximenes assembled his staff of experts at Alcalá de Henares (Complutum) for work on his great undertaking, the first Polyglot Bible, Hebrew was a language practically unknown to the clergy, and the case with Greek was not much better. The fact of the undertaking shows how strongly the need was felt.

Early in the 14th century an interesting forward step had been taken by the famous commentator, Nicolaus de Lyra. A Christian, but of Jewish parentage, he wrote a commentary on the "canonical" Bible in which he followed the Hebrew, used at first hand the Jewish exegetes, and held to the literal (not mystical, nor allegorical) meaning of the sacred text. This he followed with a commentary on the "uncanonical" scriptures, including under this title Wisdom, Sirach, Judith, Tobit, and the two books of Maccabees. His exegesis was very influential; and in 1333 he published a pamphlet with the significant title, *Tractatus de differentia nostrae translationis* (i.e., the Vulgate) *ab Hebraica veritate*. In all this there was a new emphasis which gradually gained strength in the West, and by the dawn of the 16th century was opening the eyes of the Church, far and wide, to new needs. Luther, for one, saw plainly that he must study Hebrew.[25]

The first helps to such a study had very recently appeared. Johann Reuchlin's *De Rudimentis Hebraicis*, the first Hebrew grammar and lexicon in a European tongue (in this case, Latin), was issued in 1506. Conrad Pellican's little Hebrew grammar, the fruit partly of consultation with Reuchlin and partly of his independent studies, had appeared in 1503, but it could carry the student no great distance. The important fact was that the "Hebrew verity" was now well above the horizon, and the days of the Apocrypha were really numbered, for a large part of the Christian world.

The change was a slow process, however, at first hardly noticeable. The writings in question were highly prized by all, though not all held them in the same estimation, or could agree on a single list.

The view which then prevailed throughout the Western Church was that of Augustine; though this, as was shown in the preceding pages, was not quite the same in all his writings. To the vast majority of the Christians, beyond any doubt, the O. T. scriptures contained in the Vulgate codices stood all on the same plane without any distinction. To the scholars of the Church, on the other hand, the word of Jerome had never ceased to carry great weight; we have seen, for example, how Wycliffe in the 14th century quoted his most influential dictum, and acted upon it.

Jerome pointed to the Hebrew canon, acknowledged everywhere and solely valid; yet found himself constrained by Church usage to recognize also a secondary list; and he himself translated Tobit and Judith. Augustine pointed to the outside books which the Christians for four centuries had read and cherished; but at length found himself constrained to give superior rank to those books whose authority was unquestioned. The learned leaders of the Reformation were thus provided with a doctrine of holy writ which left them in some uncertainty. Granted, moreover, the fact of a list of "secondary" authority, just what writings did it contain?

The question was pressing, and the answer could not be put off. It made trouble for all the Reformers, and even for the Roman Church. We saw, in the first pages of this historical sketch, the answer that was

25. There was this good ground for the malicious little witticism which went the rounds:

> *Si Lyra non lyrasset,*
> *Luther non saltasset.*

It was evident that others also were "dancing" to the same music.

given by the pioneer Karlstadt; also, how the list accepted by the English Church came into being. There was good reason for the uncertainty, and it continued. The Prayer of Manasseh was pushed back and forth; the Additions to Esther (Jerome's hideous arrangement) were often rejected; the apocryphal Esdras books were generally under suspicion. Luther was blamed for inconsistency in his treatment of Sirach. Third and Fourth Maccabees were generally left out of account; though the Third book is now and then included as deutero-canonical, as by Zwingli and his Swiss colleagues,[26] or as in the separate edition of the English Apocrypha which was printed in 1549.

All the Reformers recognized the secondary group of sacred books; and when the translations of the Bible in the various languages of Europe began to appear, they all contained as a matter of course the uncanonical scriptures, substantially the same list.

In the first decades of the 16th century, one and another of the great scholars of the Roman Church gave forth the same doctrine of the apocryphal writings which the Reformers were enunciating. Cardinal Ximenes, whose chief monument, the *Complutensian Polyglot* (printed in 1514–1517), has already been mentioned, uttered in its Preface the long-familiar verdict, that the books outside the canon, here printed in Greek and translated, are received by the Church rather for edification than for the establishment of doctrines.

Erasmus, whose edition of the New Testament in 1516 was the first to be published in the original Greek, was at that time inclined to doubt whether the decision of the Church in accepting certain books of the New Testament might not be questioned; and for saying this he was attacked and censured. Later, in the fourth volume of his edition of Jerome, he comes to speak of the O. T. Apocrypha, and at the outset he declares himself a true churchman, accepting whatever the authority of the Church has approved. "But," he adds, "it is of great importance to know *in what spirit* the Church approves a thing . . . . It surely does not wish Judith, Tobit, and Wisdom to have the same weight as the Pentateuch." Later still (in 1533), in an Exposition of the Creed, he gives the Hebrew canon (without Esther!) as containing the books of the Old Testament "which it would be impious to doubt"; and then goes on to say that Wisdom, Ecclesiasticus, Tobit, Judith, Esther, and the Additions to Daniel "have been received into ecclesiastical use. Whether, however, the Church receives them as possessing the same authority as the others, the spirit of the Church must know." [27] Erasmus was not quite ready to renounce all critical judgment.

Another noted scholar was more outspoken. Cardinal Cajetan, the

26. Westcott, *The Bible in the Church* (1866), pp. 269 f.
27. See Westcott, *ibid.*, pp. 252 f.

papal legate before whose tribunal Luther was summoned to appear, at Augsburg in 1518, was a stanch defender of ecclesiastical authority and a foe of the Reformers; but he and Luther could have agreed in regard to the Apocrypha. Having finished, in 1532, a commentary on "the authentic historical books" of the Old Testament—this referring solely to the Hebrew canon—Cajetan had a strong feeling of the distance existing between these writings and such others as Judith, Tobit, and the two books of Maccabees. These four and whatever others are in their class, he maintains, can be called "canonical" in a certain sense, yet they stand quite outside the *ancient* canon; and he appeals from lesser authorities and even from councils to a name almost uniquely revered by the Church, saying: "The words of councils and of doctors must alike be revised by the judgment of Jerome."

This bold saying is interesting not only as that of Luther's opponent, but also in view of its proximity to the decrees of the Council of Trent. During Cajetan's lifetime, because of the high esteem in which he was held his insistence on the final authority of Jerome was allowed to stand unchallenged; but soon after his death, which took place in 1534, his opinions were sharply criticized. Feeling was running high at that time, and it was evident that much was at stake.[28] Was the papal authority to be set aside? More than one Pope had declared all the books of the Vulgate Bible to have the same canonical rank, without regard to any limits set by the Jews.

The frequent reference to Hebrew was irritating; to the feeling of the whole western world the language of the divine oracles was the Latin; no other could possess a like sanctity. In the *Complutensian Polyglot* the Latin text occupied the center of each page, with Greek on one side and Hebrew on the other; and in the second Preface of the work this arrangement was declared to be symbolic of the relation between the Roman Church and its two chief rivals, the Greek Church and the Synagogue: "This is as Jesus was crucified between two thieves." The saying was by no means a mere pleasantry, and there were scholars who undertook to uphold in detail the authority of the inspired Vulgate against the pretensions of the corrupt and defective texts in the two rival tongues. "The thesis that the Vulgate is far closer to the original than either the Hebrew or Greek text was elaborately maintained by Morinus[29] in the early part of the seventeenth

28. Matters of doctrine were not seriously concerned. It is true that the Romanist scholars appealed to the authority of apocryphal writings for certain of their tenets (see for example Zöckler, *Die Apokryphen des A.T.,* p. 18; W. R. Churton, *Uncanonical and Apocryphal Scriptures,* p. 16); but the doctrines in question could be inferred from the canonical books.

29. Jean Morin (1591–1659), a learned and fruitful scholar, the author of important work in the Biblical field, was somewhat given to exaggeration, and this especially when refuting the Protestants.

century" (Wace's *Apocrypha*, I, xxix). Some official pronouncement on this and similar matters might well have seemed desirable.

The Council of Trent was convened by Paul III in 1545, and closed, after several interruptions, under Pius IV in 1563. In the course of the fourth session, in April, 1546, the doctrine of the Holy Scriptures was proclaimed. One important item was the decision which fixed, for the Catholic Church, the status of the disputed books. The absolute authority of the Church in this matter, as in others, was formally declared. The decree concerning the inspired scriptures of the Old Testament includes in its list the books of the Reformers' Apocrypha, interspersed among the books of the Hebrew canon, and declares all to be of equal validity for questions of doctrine. At the conclusion of the list is added: "If any one does not receive these entire books, with all their parts,[30] as they are accustomed to be read in the Catholic Church and are found in the ancient edition of the Latin Vulgate, as sacred and canonical, let him be anathema."

Three books which had been given some recognition by the early Church, and by the Protestant authorities, were left out of the Council's sacred catalogue, and yet were not wholly abandoned by the Catholics. First and Second Esdras and the Prayer of Manasseh, rejected by the Council as insufficiently attested, were eventually retained (*"ne prorsus interirent"*) in editions of the Vulgate and printed in smaller type as an Appendix, following the New Testament; thus ever since the standard (Clementine) edition of 1592; the Sixtine edition of 1590 had omitted the three books altogether.

The omission of the Prayer of Manasseh is very understandable; though the *Complutensian Polyglot* had included it, while rejecting the two Esdras books. It had only late and poor attestation, as we have seen. Second Esdras was not known to exist in Greek, besides not being included with certainty in the earlier catalogues of holy scripture, nor accepted by many of the more recent authorities. The chief reason for rejecting First Esdras seems to have been the fact that Jerome left it untranslated and spoke of it (along with Second Esdras) slightingly in the preface to his translation of Ezra and Nehemiah.

The anathema which was pronounced concerned only the rejection of the books from canonicity. It was decided, after much discussion, to add no anathema to the second part of the decree, which made the Vulgate text the final authority.

It was not easy for all the Catholic scholars to acquiesce in the rank-

30. "With all their parts" refers especially to the Additions to Daniel and Esther. By "the ancient edition" is meant Jerome's Latin Bible with the added books adopted by the early Church.

ing which the Council of Trent gave to the writings which for so long
a time and by such high authorities had been pronounced inferior. A
proposal formally made in 1566 by a noted Dominican scholar met
with some favor at the time. It was, to term "protocanonical" those
books which had never been questioned, and "deuterocanonical" the
others which the Council had certified; on the ground that the latter
were a secondary group in point of time, having received the full sanc-
tion of the Church at a late day. This proposal, however, was clearly
contrary to the Council's decree. So also were the other attempts,
which from time to time were made, to gain some freedom of individual
opinion; urging, as Erasmus and others had done, that "the Church
receives books in different ways."

The controversy over the Apocrypha now became lively, and it was
ably conducted on both sides. The designation of the Latin Vulgate as
the supreme authority in questions of the Biblical text naturally in-
censed the leaders of the Hebrew-Greek renaissance,[31] and they welcomed any opportunity, however trivial, to ridicule the irksome doctrine. In a debate at Regensburg in 1601 between Catholics and
Protestants, the latter brought forward a critical question regarding
Tobit's dog. According to the Vulgate text of 11:9, the dog expressed
his joy, as dogs do, when he reached Tobit's house: *blandimento suae
caudae gaudebat*. No Greek text, nor any other ancient version, is
known to contain this information. Here was the opening. "Did the
Divine Voice certainly say that the dog wagged his tail? Is this an
article of faith?" The question can hardly have embarrassed the
Romanists, but it delighted their opponents.

The Greek Church never came to a formal and authoritative utterance concerning the "apocryphal" books of the Greek Bible. The
tendency for a long time seems to have been to follow the teaching of
Athanasius, who rejected them as uncanonical; permitting them to be
read to catechumens, however. Gradually the tide turned the other
way, since all the scriptures alike were "Church books," and there was
little discussion of the question of relative rank. The decision of Trent
added its potent influence.

In the 17th century controversy arose, and continued for some time.
Cyril Lucar, Patriarch of Constantinople in 1621–1637, had imbibed
Protestant doctrines, and aimed to reform the Eastern Church on
Calvinistic lines. He accepted, and proclaimed in his *Confession of
Faith*, the Reformers' view of the apocryphal scriptures. This en-
croachment from the West met with strong opposition. A synod at

31. Luther had died on February 18, 1546, a few days after his articles on Holy
Scripture and Tradition had been brought forward for discussion at the Council of
Trent.

Jaffa in 1642 upheld the canonicity of the troublesome books; and the *Orthodox Confession of the Catholic and Apostolic Eastern Church*, drawn up in 1643 by the Metropolitan of Kiev, took the same ground. The influence of Cyril [32] and his followers was powerful, nevertheless; and in 1672 was convened the Synod of Jerusalem, which was directed chiefly against "the party of the Calvinists." The doctrine of the Synod in regard to the O. T. canon was practically the same as that of the Council of Trent, and it eventually held the field. In the Eastern churches the Biblical books are all given the same authority; while for the learned among the clergy there is obviously possible a certain freedom of opinion, if only because of the debate among high officials of the Church in the 17th century.

§8. THE CONTROVERSIES OVER THE USE OF THE APOCRYPHA

IN all parts of the Western Church, at the beginning of the 17th century, the status of a fairly definite portion of the "outside books" seemed to be settled. The members of the smaller group—members by virtue of their long inclusion in the Church's sacred scripture—had been given a well understood rank. By the Romanists they were put on the same plane as the Law and the Prophets. By the Protestants they were given a standing which was something more than toleration; on the one side denial of divine authority, but on the other side a rank above the mass of apocrypha, and the practice of reading from them in the public worship. Especially, they seemed to have the assurance of a secure place in all the printed Bibles, Catholic or Protestant.

As new translations of the Scriptures now appeared, in rapid succession, in the various languages of Europe, German, French, Dutch, English, Italian, Spanish, Scandinavian, and still others, the familiar apocryphal books were in every case included or planned for, as a matter of course. Being read in the language of the people, they became more familiar than ever. Also, because they were now put in a place by themselves, fenced off, as it were, from the canonical books, their lower rank was made more conspicuous than it had ever been in the past. No reader of the Catholic Bible would henceforth see divine authority in the two "Esdras" books and the Prayer of Manasseh; nor would Protestants, except by occasional inadvertence, quote their Apocrypha as holy scripture. Just as in the early centuries *the codex* had guaranteed to these particular books enduring recognition by the Church, so now *the printed Bible* assured to them, for all the future, an inferior place in the public estimation.

32. He was murdered in 1637 by the Janissaries under orders from the Sultan Murad.

A more important factor, in the period of Church history now beginning, was the new emphasis on the doctrine of inspiration. In proportion as the authentic Bible was felt to be the very Word of God, the only source of true Christian doctrine and guide-book of Christian life, the interval separating canonical from uncanonical was bound to widen. In fact, the time soon came when uneasiness was felt and expressed, here and there, over the too close association of the holy with the profane.

The earliest and most persistent objections to the public use of the Apocrypha were made in England. The English Lectionary, while making no use of the books of Maccabees and the three books banned by the Council of Trent, included all the others with hardly any change or curtailment. Even in the reign of Elizabeth the Puritans had assailed the public reading of these inferior and "frivolous" writings; and in the 17th and 18th centuries the polemic against their presence in the church services became increasingly sharp and widespread. Various attempts to get rid of this or that especially obnoxious portion were made. Thus at the Hampton Court Conference (1604) Bel and the Dragon and the unsavory portions of Tobit were removed from the Lectionary; only to be dragged in again, almost entire, at the unfortunate Savoy Conference of 1661. Also in 1604 the whole twenty-sixth chapter of Ecclesiasticus (Sirach) was omitted from the Prayer Book (as well as the single verse 46:20, with its allusion to the Witch of Endor), and in the revision under Charles II half of the twenty-fifth chapter was likewise left out.

There was at first no serious attempt to remove the unholy group altogether from the sacred Book, though as early as 1629 an edition of the Bible "without the Apocrypha" was published in London; while in 1549 an English version of the Apocrypha (including Third Maccabees) had been printed separately. But more than one urgent proposal was made to take the group out from its undeserved position between the two Testaments and put it in a humbler place.

Protestant scholars on the Continent, especially the Dutch, were also exercised about this matter, and at the Synod of Dort (1618–1619) discussions relating to the Apocrypha had a prominent place. It was finally voted, to permit a translation of the Apocrypha to be included in the Dutch Bible, but only under certain conditions: the group must be put at the end of the Bible, after the New Testament and with a space between; it must be printed in smaller type, separately paged, and given a special title; also furnished with marginal notes calling attention to each divergence from doctrines of the canonical scriptures. "Jewish legends and inventions" were blemishes specially mentioned at Dort in the characterization of these "merely human books."

In 1643 the famous English scholar John Lightfoot preached before the House of Commons a sermon which has been widely quoted in works dealing with the canon. From his Talmudic and Midrashic studies he had gained a rather low opinion of Jewish popular literature, and he would give it no place in Holy Scripture. Especially irksome to him was the way in which this uncanonical group, from its position, gave the false impression of forming a link between the two Testaments, though having no true connection with either of them. The two would join beautifully, he said, as they were divinely intended, if it were not that "the wretched Apocrypha," "this patchery of human invention," is now thrust in between them. He would remove and cast away this obstacle. The Westminster Assembly, which was convened at just this time, took the same attitude (Lightfoot was one of the original members of the Assembly). The third article of the Westminster Confession declares that the apocryphal books are "of no authority in the Church of God, nor to be otherwise approved *or made use of* than other human writings."

A succession of noted scholars of the Church of England urged the retention of the ancient custom; the worth of which, they said, had been abundantly proved. They expressed apprehension lest this literature, so important historically, should fall into utter neglect. The opposition, however, gained in force and extent, and the attack on the offending scriptures was unceasing. In the last conference at the Jerusalem Chamber in 1689 there was a proposal, vehemently debated, to omit from the calendar all lessons from the Apocrypha. The following century saw increasing clashes.

Stories which had been "useful for instruction" while they could still be believed true lost the most of their religious value in the later day when they came to be critically estimated. Popular wisdom which had been reverenced as ancient church doctrine even if not directly inspired, could become very irksome when persistently derided. The omission from the Prayer Book of certain chapters of Ecclesiasticus has already been mentioned. Ben Sira, for some reason, had a low opinion of womankind and felt free to express it. "All wickedness is but little to the wickedness of a woman" (25:19). "Of woman was the beginning of sin, and through her we all die" (25:24). "As the climbing up a sandy way is to the feet of the aged, so is a wife full of words to a quiet man" (25:20). As homely proverbs uttered with a smile, such sayings would trouble no one; but when regularly read in the church service, as a part of sacred scripture, they became intolerable. Several of the recorded complaints mention Tobit's dog; others, very naturally, the demon Asmodeus; the "putid fable" of Bel and the Dragon is now and again held up to ridicule. Small matters; but it was the constant touching of a sore spot.

The British and Foreign Bible Society,[33] founded in 1804, was accustomed from the first to give aid to the circulation of the Bible on the Continent through the affiliated societies, Swiss, German, Swedish, etc. (eighteen were founded between 1804 and 1814). The beginning was made with the scriptures (mainly Luther's German Bible) that were issued at low cost by the famous Canstein Institute at Halle. Other languages followed. All these Bibles contained the Apocrypha, and this fact brought the British Society under sharp criticism, especially from its auxiliary branches in Edinburgh and Glasgow. This reached such a pitch that in 1811 it was decided to ask the Continental societies to leave out the Apocrypha from the Bibles which they circulated with the British aid. The request met with a strong protest, and was so evidently futile that two years later it was withdrawn. Energetic attempts were now made to adopt for the Society a policy definitely opposed to the publication of these "uninspired writings." A majority of the directors wished to take this course, but the resulting outcry on the Continent, especially in Germany, Austria, and Sweden, restrained them from taking the desired action.

A new bone of contention appeared in 1819. A subvention was granted for the publication in the three languages, Italian, Spanish, and Portuguese, of a Roman Catholic Bible—containing of course the disputed books interspersed as canonical among the other O. T. scriptures! The result was what might have been expected. In addition to bitter criticism in England, the Scotch societies declared the action a breach of contract. After long deliberation the British Society decided (1822) on a middle course, devoting its funds only to the distribution of the canonical scriptures, while leaving the auxiliaries free to print and publish the uncanonical books at their own expense. The announcement of this policy, and a notorious example of its operation, increased the bitterness of the controversy; and in December, 1824, the directors voted to rescind the former action, and in future to aid in the publication of Bibles containing the apocryphal books only in case the latter were printed as an Appendix to the canonical books. This, again, added fuel to the fire.

In the following year the Edinburgh branch society sent its ultimatum to London: either the British and Foreign Bible Society must cease, entirely and finally, from distributing the Apocrypha, or else the Scottish societies must withdraw their support. Apart from other unfortunate consequences of such a secession, the fact that the contribution of the Scotch auxiliaries to the funds of the parent society had averaged considerably over five thousand pounds a year made the

---

33. For a detailed history of the events now to be mentioned, see G. Browne, *History of the British and Foreign Bible Society*, I (1859), 94–101, 360 ff.

Edinburgh note a very formidable document. The Society could not well dispense with the support of Scotland; but on the other hand how could it afford to take a step which would probably result in lopping off the important continental branches? The controversy waxed hot, and continued unabated until 1826, when the adherents of the stricter praxis won the day. All action taken with reference to the Apocrypha since 1811 had already been stricken from the records, and now the Society formally adopted a rule against the circulation of the troublesome group of writings: "The Principles of the Society exclude the circulation of those Books, or parts of Books, which are usually termed Apocryphal." This action was formally announced in May, 1827.

There were two chief consequences. In the first place, a storm of protest arose on the Continent, and the affiliated societies, now numbering about fifty, cut loose from the parent organization, and thereafter went their own way. In the second place, the Scotchmen, whose blood was up, now demanded the immediate removal of all those officers of the Bible Society who had stood on the side of the Apocrypha. This being refused, they also announced their secession, and an independent Bible Society in Edinburgh was forthwith founded.

The story of this controversy, as it concerns the attitude of the continental scholars toward the Apocrypha, illustrates the difference between their doctrine of the scriptures and that of their colleagues in the British Isles. When the emissaries from the London society made the round of the Swiss and German auxiliaries, in 1811, with the aim of discontinuing the circulation of the Apocrypha, they found everywhere a theory of degrees of inspiration which baffled them. The Protestant churches on the Continent never carried the distinction between "canonical" and "uncanonical" scriptures as far as it was carried in England and Scotland.

It was chiefly as a result of the British agitation, however, that a lively controversy over the Apocrypha arose on the Continent, and especially in Germany, in the middle of the 19th century.[34] The question was generally not whether the deuterocanonical books should be suppressed, but rather, what value should be assigned to them. A majority of the foremost scholars emphasized the historical importance of these later and humbler writings, and held that selections from them were desirable for public reading—in all this repeating what had been said a generation earlier by many of the best British scholars. Both parties to the controversy in Germany and the neighboring countries recognized in Old Testament and New Testament a divine revela-

34. For a concise account of the debate and its results see Zöckler, *Die Apokryphen,* pp. 20-22.

tion; and the difference in point of view between those who rather violently urged the rejection of the "profane inventions" from all further use, and the Austrian pastor who declared, about 1850 (W. Canton, *History of the British and Foreign Bible Society*, II, 224), that he would not suffer a Bible without the Apocrypha to remain under his roof, was hardly as wide as the language used would indicate. The debate on the Continent brought about scarcely any change of policy in the matter of printing and distributing the disputed books.

The American Bible Society, which was founded at New York in 1816 [35] under the influence of the London Society, followed with keen interest the controversy over the Apocrypha, and was confirmed in its own policy by the result. The Bibles which it issued never contained the objectionable books, and the latter were more and more rarely seen, whether in American or in English editions.

Both in England and in the United States the use of the Apocrypha in the church services dwindled to a small amount. In England at the time of the Reformation the lessons from these books were appointed to be read on week-days only, during two months of the year. The books thus included have already been specified, in the preceding pages, where also was mentioned the fact of certain changes made in the 17th century. In the revision of the Lectionary in 1867, the time during which such lessons were read was reduced from two months to three weeks; all historical or quasi-historical books were dropped. Thus only Baruch (a small portion), Wisdom, and Ecclesiasticus were left, and even these were only represented by short selections. In the American Church the situation is the same. Aside from four lessons on Saints' days, the readings from the Apocrypha are confined to the month of November. Baruch and Tobit are represented, each by a single lesson. Otherwise, the lessons through the greater part of November are from Ecclesiasticus (chiefly) and Wisdom.

The "Church books" of the Fathers are still in evidence, but in the light and heat of modern times and historical studies the recognition of their religious value to the layman has reached a point which is perhaps its lowest ebb.

35. It had a predecessor, The Bible Society of Philadelphia, founded in 1808.

PART II
SPECIAL INTRODUCTION

§9. Literature

THE following standard works cover the field of O. T. Apocrypha.

O. F. Fritzsche u. W. Grimm, *Kurzgefasstes exegetisches Handbuch zu den Apokryphen des A.T.* (1851–1860), by far the most extensive and thorough commentary. H. Wace, *The Speaker's Commentary, The Apocrypha,* 2 vols. (1888) chiefly useful for the historical Introductions. O. Zöckler, *Die Apokryphen des A.T.* (1891), translations, including a number of the "pseudepigrapha"). E. Kautzsch, *Die Apokryphen u. Pseudepigraphen des A.T.,* 2 Bde. (1900), reprinted in 1921. R. H. Charles, *The Apocrypha and Pseudepigrapha of the Old Testament,* 2 vols. (1913). E. Schürer, *Geschichte des jüdischen Volkes* (4te Auflage, 1909), III, 188–716 (with full references to the literature). Hastings, *Dictionary of the Bible* (1898–1904). Cheyne-Black, *Encyclopaedia Biblica* (1899–1903). *The Jewish Encyclopedia* (1901–1905). The volume in the *Variorum Bible* containing the Apocrypha, edited by C. J. Ball (1892) is useful. Fritzsche's *Libri Apocryphi Vet. Test.* (1871), is comprehensive and convenient, though the text is not always trustworthy.

§10. First Esdras

THE fragment called "First Esdras" [36] has been the most thoroughly misunderstood document in the entire apocryphal literature. It is regarded on all hands, down to the present day, as a "book," and many are the conjectures as to the purpose and plan of its "author" in making this peculiar compilation. It consists, in the main, of material contained in the Chronicler's history, that is, of portions of Chronicles, Ezra, and Nehemiah. There is also an episode of some length which interrupts the Biblical account and is not found elsewhere. The remarkable problems which it presents may be seen in the following synopsis of its contents.

The beginning is made with the last two chapters of Second Chronicles, chapter 35 with its account of Josiah's passover, and of the death of the king in the battle at Megiddo, and chapter 36 with the subsequent history of the Judean kingdom down to the Babylonian captivity. All this corresponds throughout to the canonical text, except in 1 Esd. 1:21 f. (Eng. version, 23 f.), see below, and in the omission

36. Also called Third Ezra, the Greek Ezra, the Apocryphal Ezra, and even Second Ezra (the "First" being Ezra-Nehemiah).

of the closing words of 2 Chron. 36:22 f., verbally repeated in the book of Ezra, introducing Cyrus and his proclamation. Then comes the first chapter of Ezra, telling of the preparation made under Cyrus for a return to Jerusalem.

Thereupon follows an astonishing example of history stood on its head, in the correspondence between the enemies of Judah and the Persian kings Xerxes (Ahasuerus) and Artaxerxes,[37] Ezra 4:6–24. The Jews are still in Babylonia, but the official letters declare them to be building the walls of Jerusalem.

Here enters the foreign episode mentioned above, the Story of the Three Young Guardsmen and their lively debate at the court of the great king; chapters 3 and 4 of First Esdras and verses 1–6 of chapter 5. This bit of "wisdom literature" will be treated separately. Its original language was Aramaic, as has been abundantly proved. Immediately after it, *and given essential connection with it*, is the account of the return of the exiles under Cyrus; the same account, exactly, which is given in the second chapter of the canonical Ezra. The great king of this episode is named Darius, and the significance of this fact will be considered presently.

Following the account of the return to Jerusalem comes the history contained in Ezra, chapters 3–10, unchanged except for the omission of the official correspondence and its effect, in 4:6–24, which had already been given another setting, see above. The history in First Esdras is thus carried as far as 9:36, corresponding to Ezra 10:44.

Here begins a most important variation, for 1 Esd. 9:37 corresponds to Neh. 7:73; and the remainder of its ninth chapter, through 9:35 where it ends in the middle of a clause, is the story of the reading of the law by Ezra, given in Neh. 8:1–12, with also the first words of verse 13. Thus First Esdras ends with an unfinished sentence in an unfinished narrative.

Now the leap from Ezra 10 to Nehemiah 8 is not a new thing. We see exactly the same order of chapters in Josephus, *Antt.*, 11, v, 4 f., section 4 ending with the equivalent of Ezra 10:44 and section 5 continuing immediately with Neh. 7:73 and 8:1 ff. And this is not all. It might seem easily possible that two independent versions of this history should give Nehemiah 8 the above connection, since it plainly belongs to the story of Ezra; he was sent to Jerusalem *to bring the law* (Ezra 7:14, 25 f.), and here he introduces it! But another explanation is needed when it is seen that Josephus's history contains also the *other* peculiar feature of First Esdras, the episode of the Three Young Guardsmen at the court of Darius. This is given in the same form in

---

37. Ahasuerus has been lost from our text, but the array of proper names in 1 Esd. 2:15 shows that Ezra 4:6 was originally included.

Antt. 11, chapters i–iii; the story is preceded, as in First Esdras, by the misplaced section; and there is the same curious transition to the return under Cyrus.[38]

The explanation is that here, as in every other part of the sacred history, Josephus follows his one prime authority, the Greek Bible.

Note the following facts.—1. First Esdras is simply an unchanged extract from the old ("Septuagint") version of Chronicles-Ezra-Nehemiah which is known to have been in existence in the middle of the 2d century B.C.—2. Our present Greek version, traditionally known as "the LXX," is that of Theodotion, of the 2d century A.D.—3. The Hebrew-Aramaic text which Theodotion rendered, the text of our present Hebrew Bible, is one from which the Story of the Three Guardsmen and its sequel had recently been cut out.—4. When the excision was made, *18 verses of the Chronicler's original narrative* were cut out, of necessity. They appear in 1 Esd. 4:47b–56, 62 f., 5:1–6, and originally followed Ezra 1:11.—5. At the beginning of the present era there was probably no text of the Chronicler's history in existence which did not contain the episode of the guardsmen and make Nehemiah 8 the sequel of Ezra 10.—6. The fragment called First Esdras was rescued from a Greek codex, and given a separate existence, with the purpose of saving an old and interesting variant version of the history. We have it in its original extent.[39]

Since First Esdras is merely an extract saved from the older LXX, why is it so obviously a torso? or, to put the question in another way, what determined the limits of our "book"? Why was the beginning not made with 2 Chron. 34, the reign of Josiah, with the necessary antecedents of his celebration of the passover? Or, if the purpose was merely to include a portion of Chronicles, why was not 2 Chron. 36:17, the reign of Zedekiah, not chosen as the best starting point? And, much more remarkable, why does the "book" end in the middle of a sentence? when there could be no doubt whatever, from Neh. 8:13, how the sentence ended.[40]

The following seems to be a natural explanation. At some time in the 2d century A.D., after the "foreign episode" had been excised from the book of Ezra, some one (possibly a Christian but more likely a Jew) plucked out from a Greek codex containing Chronicles-Ezra-

38. Josephus indeed experiments with a new series of Persian kings (his own device), but only makes a bad matter worse.

39. The above facts were ascertained and set forth, for the first time, by the present writer in various publications of the years 1897, 1907 and 1908, afterward collected in *Ezra Studies*. See also "The Chronicler's History of the Return under Cyrus," *Am. Jour. Sem. Langs.*, *37* (Jan., 1921), 81–100.

40. The Lucianic recension, the "L-text," ed. Lagarde, fills out the sentence, quite arbitrarily.

Nehemiah the portion, probably two quires, which covered the time-honored version of the history, now superseded. There was no thought of creating a formal document; the purpose was merely to preserve for a time something interesting which seemed likely to be lost. The portion needing to be rescued extended from the first chapter of Ezra through the book and thereafter far enough in Nehemiah 8 to show plainly that this chapter had been counted as belonging to the book of Ezra. This much of the text was necessary, no more was needed. The first quire happened to begin exactly at 2 Chron. 35:1, and the last quire happened to end with the first two words of Neh. 8:13. There was no need of finishing the sentence, or of continuing with the rest of the chapter; on the contrary, it was important to make plain the fact of a mere fragment.

When the Christians made up their own codices of the O. T. scriptures, this variant version of the Ezra history came to their notice and naturally aroused much interest. They adopted it as it stood, designating it as *First* Esdras since it evidently would be out of place after the story of Nehemiah.

It is important to ascertain, if possible, how the Chronicler's history was continued, in the codex from which this long extract was taken. This was the accepted version, apparently the only one in use in the 1st century A.D. What, may we suppose, followed the account of Ezra's reading of the law, here appended to Ezra 10? Josephus, our only external witness, proceeds directly with the book of Nehemiah, giving the substance of the first six chapters and making brief but plain allusion to 7:4, 11:1, 12:27, and 13:10 f. Of chapters 9 and 10 he makes no use. It has plausibly been conjectured that these two chapters were transposed to the book of Ezra along with chapter 8 (thus in *Ezra Studies*, pp. 31 f.), and this theory seems most probable. The only portion of the text of Nehemiah *requiring* to be transposed was the story of Ezra's public reading. Its connection with chapter 9 is by no means close; and the interpolation of Nehemiah's name in 10:2 (especially), which must have been made soon after these chapters were given their present place,[41] might seem sufficient to keep the two chapters 9 and 10 from being appended to the story of Ezra. But

41. The original order of the Ezra narrative is as follows: Ezra, chaps. 7 and 8; Neh., chap. 7:70–73 and chap. 8; Ezra, chaps. 9 and 10; Neh., chaps. 9 and 10. This order was established and demonstrated, for the first time, by the present writer in his *Composition and Historical Value of Ezra-Nehemiah* (1896), published as a Beiheft of the *Zeitschr. f. d. alttest. Wissenschaft*, p. 34. The entire Ezra history in its original sequence was printed in the *Am. Jour. Sem. Langs.*, July 1909, and in *Ezra Studies*, pp. 265–278; where also the attempt was made (pp. 255–258) to show in detail how the great confusion was first brought about by the remarkable resemblance (almost word for word!) of Neh. 7:70–73a and 73b–8:1 to Ezra 2:68–70 and 3:1. The Chronicler is fond of repeating himself; compare with these two passages also 1 Chron. 29:6–8.

the interpolation was made in 8:9 as well as in 10:2, and probably at about the same time. Moreover, since the Chronicler made Ezra and Nehemiah contemporaries, it is quite conceivable that an Ezra narrative should mention Nehemiah in advance of his proper history. A sentence in Josephus, *Antt.*, 11, v, 8, seems important: "When Nehemiah saw that the city was thinly populated, he urged the Priests and the Levites to leave the country and remove to the city." The first part of the sentence refers to 7:4, and the latter part to 11:1; and this suggests that in the Greek text employed by Josephus Neh. 7 was immediately followed by chapter 11 (as originally was the case!).

Again, the date in Neh. 9:1 *appears* to give close connection with Neh. 8, in which the last date (end of vs. 18) is the 22nd of Tishri. The "24th day of this month" in 9:1 really means the month Nisan, referring to Ezra 10:17; but this fact is not apparent. Neh. 10 is inseparable from chapter 9; and it would have been obvious to any editor or scribe that Neh. 7:72 could not have been immediately followed by 9:1!

The conclusion is, that the three chapters, Neh. 8–10, were regarded (mistakenly) as continuous, and *in this version*, Hebrew as well as Greek, were appended as a single block of narrative to the book of Ezra. Then followed Neh. 1:1–7:72, 11:1–13:31.

There are still questions to be answered relating to the incorporation of the Story of the Three Guardsmen in the account of the Return. The view has been held and defended that the Chronicler himself gave the story its present place, and notice must be taken of this hypothesis. Another question is more important: On what theory of early Persian history did the borrower of the story plant it in the middle of the first chapter of Ezra with confidence that it would be permitted to remain there? These matters can best be discussed in connection with the story itself, and they therefore are reserved for the next section.

It was mentioned, above, that the two verses 1 Esd. 1:21 f. (Engl. trans., pp. 23 f.) are a peculiar feature of this version. They present in fact a problem of interest and difficulty, for they are the sole remnant of a passage which has been lost from the original text of Chronicles. There was at this point a brief passage effecting the transition from the story of Josiah's passover (ending at 2 Chron. 35:20) to the account (beginning at vs. 21) of his defiance of Pharaoh Neco and his death at Megiddo. In our present Hebrew text there is only an allusion to some such paragraph in the first words of verse 21: "After all this which Josiah did *in setting the temple in order*." In the standard Greek (Theodotion's trans., 2d century A.D.) the gap is filled by a passage, four verses, taken bodily from 2 Kings 23:24–27. The fact appears to have remained unnoticed that this borrowing took place *in the Hebrew* which Theodotion rendered, the text differing slightly from that which was translated in Kings. The Greek of First Esdras, the only witness to the original reading of Chronicles, seems to show that the Hebrew of the passage had suffered such damage that it was found necessary to cut it out altogether.

To summarize: First Esdras does not represent the original form of this portion of the Chronicler's history, but a popular revision consisting partly of interpolation and partly of rearrangement. Our text of this revised form is derived from a rescued Greek fragment (now called "First Esdras"), but the same text in the same arrangement throughout existed in Semitic, partly Hebrew, partly Aramaic, the Greek being a good translation. This seems, moreover, to have been the *only* form of the Chronicler's history which was in circulation in the 1st century A.D., whether in Semitic or in Greek. Our canonical text of Ezra-Nehemiah was formed in the 2d century A.D., partly by excision of the story and its appendages, partly by rearrangement. It does not give us all that the Chronicler wrote, but the rest can be restored.

Several matters which must be discussed before chapters 2–5 can be understood will be treated in the following section in connection with the interpolation of the story. In particular, the proceeding of the interpolator, whose view of Medo-Persian history was the one then generally accepted, and the fact that the present intolerable confusion *is due to a later editor*, have not been understood. See §11.

Literature. See §9; also "The Nature and Origin of First Esdras," *Am. Jour. Sem. Langs., 23* (1907), 116–141 (the first recognition of the true nature of the "book"), reprinted in *Ezra Studies.* S. Tedesche, *A Critical Edition of I Esdras,* 1928 (the best edition of the Greek text). H. C. York, "The Latin Versions of First Esdras," *Am. Jour. Sem. Langs., 26* (1910), 253–302.

§11. The Story of the Three Guardsmen

The tale of the three young guardsmen at the court of Darius is a fine bit of oriental wisdom. The part which it has been made to play in Jewish history is briefly indicated in the section dealing with First Esdras, where it is treated as an interpolation in a context not suited to contain it. By some potent hand, and on some potent theory, it was pushed into the middle of the Chronicler's story of the return of "all Israel" from Babylonia to Jerusalem *under Cyrus!* In the fragment known as "First Esdras" the story, with its appendages, occupies a considerable portion, chapters 3:1–5:6. For the basal facts regarding the origin and character of this version of the Chronicler's narrative, see the preceding section.

The subject is an old favorite, a contest of wits held in the presence of a king or prince who bestows a reward. King Darius is in a heavy sleep after a "great feast," [42] and the three young men who constitute his bodyguard take the opportunity to prepare a diversion for the monarch and his courtiers. They will hold a debate on the question, What thing is mightiest? So each of the three writes his answer on a slip of papyrus, and seals it with his own seal. The youths also make bold to propose the reward of the victor: he whose answer the king and the three princes of Persia shall judge the wisest shall be given splendid gifts and honors (duly specified), and shall be permitted to sit beside the king and be called his cousin. This also is put in writing, and together with the three slips is put under the king's pillow. When the king awakes, they agree, he shall be shown these writings.

The story of course assumes that Darius will be glad to confirm all this when he has the opportunity, and eventually, in 4:42, we are told that he did so.

The contest came off according to the plan. The first had written, Wine is mightiest. He proceeds to show how the wine overpowers its victim, body and mind, and how it turns human affairs and conditions upside down. The man, whether noble or slave, is made to do strange things, and when he becomes sober he has no recollection of them. "O sirs, is not wine the mightiest thing?"

The second had written, The king is mightiest; and he now sets forth the powers of the absolute monarch. At his word of command men build cities, or destroy them. If he wishes to make war, they give their lives in his service. In time of peace they bring him tribute. No one disobeys him; is not he the most powerful?

The third had written, Women are mightiest; *but above all things Truth bears away the victory*. (This seems hardly fair; the agreement was that each should name "one thing," ἕνα λόγον. Why should this contestant have two strings to his bow? since there was no obvious connection between women and truth. For an answer, see below.)

He began: The king is great, and wine is strong, but without women they could not exist. Of women men are born, brought up, and clothed; by women they are ruled. A man heaps up gold and jewels; he sees a beautiful woman, and is lost, and his money is lost. I myself saw the

---

42. By a patent mistranslation our Greek text declares that the king "retired to his bed *and awoke*," though this is flatly contradicted in the next few verses.

king's concubine snatch the crown from his head and slap his face; he could only gape at her, and was completely at her service. O sirs, are not women mighty, since they wield such power?

He proceeded to speak of truth: Great is the earth, high are the heavens, swift is the sun in his course; but earth and heaven and all its powers magnify truth. They totter and tremble, but truth is steadfast. The wine, the king, the women, the children of men and all their works must perish, but truth abides. Hers is the kingdom, and the power, and the glory, for ever. Blessed is the God of truth.

The people all shouted, Great is truth, and it prevails! The king said to the youth, Ask what you will, above what was written, and it is yours. You shall sit next me, and shall be called my cousin.

It seems plain enough, even from the foregoing abstract of the story, that it is not a Jewish composition, but a characteristic piece of pagan literature. The way in which it has been fitted into a Jewish historical context is interesting, and is more instructive than has been generally realized. By means of skillful interpolation and adaptation the successful contestant at the court of "Darius" is shown to have been a Jew; and the reward which he receives "above what was written" is made to play an important part in the return of the exiles from Babylonia.

In the first place, there is the obvious insertion in 4:13, the parenthetic *"this was Zerubbabel,"* just after the mention of the third contestant. Who this Zerubbabel was (for no such name had been mentioned in the history), the reader is left to guess. The name is not repeated, however; in 4:58 he is simply "the young man."

The real work of incorporating the story in the Chronicler's history begins when the account of the contest is ended. The insertion of such a foreign-sounding episode would require a formal connection, on either side, both firm and plausible; and this might well seem impossible of accomplishment. An event taking place under the eye of "Darius" is here framed *also* in the reign of Cyrus. Were there two great Persian kings reigning at one and the same time? This, as will be seen, creates no difficulty. Again, there is the astonishing transposition which "stands the history on its head," 2:16–30, making the sequence of the kings to be Cyrus, Artaxerxes, Darius, Cyrus. It can now be shown that this transposition was the work of a later hand; the man who interpolated the story could not, and did not, thus destroy his own work.

It was observed in the preceding chapter that the story *is given essential connection with the history* into which it has been dovetailed. This fact, which seems never to have been rightly apprehended, is of fundamental importance for the understanding of this portion of First Esdras. The dovetailing, which for the most part is easy to recognize, is in the latter part of the interpolation, after the account of the debate. The beginning, on the contrary, is made abruptly.

The first chapter of Ezra was cut in two at the end of the eleventh verse, which gives the number of the vessels of gold and silver which Cyrus delivered to Sheshbazzar, *the Persian governor of Judea.*[43] Thereupon followed immediately the story of Darius and the debate held at his court. When this was finished, at 4:42, a patch in Aramaic (the language of the story) made the connection with the return of the exiles. In this patch the victorious guardsman reminds Darius that he had promised to send to Jerusalem the vessels *which Cyrus had set apart for the purpose.* Darius, this means, is the supreme ruler of the Medes and Persians (3:1, cf. Dan. 6:1, 29, 9:1, 10:1, 11:1), reigning in Susa, while Cyrus is his vice-gerent in Babylon. This is said again, with the utmost clearness, in 4:57: "He (Darius) sent away also all the vessels from Babylon that Cyrus had set apart; and all that Cyrus had given in commandment, the same charged he also to be done." (Any dealing with outside provinces must, according to the interpolator, be by order of the supreme ruler.) Both Darius and Cyrus, it is here said (vss. 43–46), had vowed, at the time when they attacked Babylon, to send the precious vessels back to Jerusalem, and to build the Jews' temple.[44] Observe, moreover, that the debate of the three guardsmen took place *at Susa;* for we are told in 4:61 that the youth took the letters from Darius and *brought them to Babylon;* that is, he was to deliver them to Cyrus.[45]

These letters, written in the name of Cyrus by the Chronicler, originally followed the eleventh verse of the first chapter of Ezra. Written in Hebrew and occupying ten verses, they are now preserved only in translation, in 1 Esd. 4:47b–56. An attempt to restore the original Hebrew text was made in *Ezra Studies*, pp. 125–128.

Next came the interpolator's second patch, 4:57–61, telling how

43. 1 Esd. 2:11 has the correct translation, as I have shown elsewhere; see *Jour. Am. Or. Soc., 43* (1923), 234 f. Our English version is wrong.

44. The vows of both were officially fulfilled; see not only 1 Esd. 4:51 but also Ezra 5:16, the foundations laid by the Persian governor; and 6:2, the official order deposited *in Media.*

45. The view of Medo-Persian history presented here so plainly by the Jewish interpolator was the standard Jewish doctrine in the last three centuries B.C. Darius Hystaspis, as "Darius the Mede," was believed to have preceded Cyrus; thus also in Daniel (both halves of the book) and in Ezra. The Chronicler, who wastes no time, had no reason to mention Darius the Mede and the Medo-Persian coalition; but the fact that he made Cyrus to be followed by Ahasuerus (Xerxes) and then proceeded with *The Persian kings in their true relative order from Artaxerxes I to Darius III* (Neh. 12:22), shows that his view was the same as that held by the others. They were all learned men. See also the section on Tobit, at the end.

Darius ratified the plans of Cyrus, and how the youth took the letters
to Babylon. These five verses were probably written in Hebrew, the
language of the preceding and following contexts, but they may have
been Aramaic. With verse 62 the Chronicler's narrative, concluding
the first chapter of Ezra, is resumed, and from this point on it is continued without interruption.

The plan of the interpolator, to make the restoration of Israel a
joint project of Darius and Cyrus, was well conceived and skillfully
executed. The "vows" of the two great kings, made in mutual understanding, are briefly mentioned but made conspicuous (4:43–46). The
two editorial patches, 4:43–47a and 57–61, are admirable in effective-
ness and in economy of material. In the case of each of these insertions
the connection on either side is perfect and the transition wholly
natural. This was a redactor of more than ordinary ability.

The passage 5:1–6 originally formed the beginning of the second
chapter of Ezra. So a number of scholars have held (see Ewald, *Gesch.
des Volkes Israel*, 1851 ff., IV, 111, and Bertheau-Ryssel, *Handbuch
zum A.T.*, 1887, Ezra-Neh., pp. 12 ff.), recognizing these verses as
originally Hebrew, while supposing the preceding narrative to have
been composed in Greek. The passage gives *the date* of the great expedition and *the names of its leaders*. The text has suffered important
change in three places: 1. The change of "Cyrus" to "Darius" in
verse 2; 2. the insertion, "who spoke wise sentences before Darius the
king of Persia," in verse 6; 3. the words "Joakim the son of" in verse
5. The last-named of these three false readings is merely the result of
a carelessly read or written Hebrew text, *we-yōqīm ben,* "and Joakim
the son of," instead of *wa-yāqām bō,* "and there rose up with him."
See *Jour. Bib. Lit.* (1897), p. 170; *Ezra Studies*, p. 28.

The other two changes are much more significant. They are deliberate alterations, each supporting the other, and it is plain that they
cannot have been made by the interpolator of the story, whose Darius
certainly authorizes a return of the Jews *under Cyrus!* [46] The explanation of the alterations can hardly be in doubt when they are
taken in connection with the strange removal of Ezra 4:6–24 to the
place which it occupies in 1 Esd., 2:16–30; a transposition which (as
was remarked above) cannot have been the work of our interpolator.

On the contrary, we have here the hasty and ill-considered work of
an editor who saw in this "Darius" the *Persian* king named in Ezra
5:1 ff., Darius Nothus, in whose reign Zerubbabel "began to build the
house of God." It was *this* editor who conceived the bright idea of mak-

46. This is twice clearly said, in 4:44, 57, in perfect agreement with 1:10–15 and
5:55, 71–73.

ing Zerubbabel the victor in the royal presence; he it was who inserted "this was Zerubbabel" in 4:13; who made the alterations in 5:2, 6, and transposed the section above mentioned, thus making the great expedition take place under a king several reigns later than Cyrus.[47] The result was the *chaos* which we see before us in the first five chapters of our First Esdras; and this in turn brought about the excision which left a noticeable gap between chapters 1 and 2 in our book of Ezra. The portion cut out included all of 1 Esd. 3:1–5:6 (18 verses of the Chronicler's own composition went with it); and the correspondence under Ahasuerus and Artaxerxes I was of course restored to its proper place.

Several matters concerning the original form of the Story of the Three Guardsmen have yet to be considered. One of these relates to the supposed scene of the contest, and to the identity of the king who was first intended.

The proper names in 4:29 have led many students of First Esdras (including the present writer, in *Ezra Studies*, pp. 40 f.) to look for a real historical scene; but only doubtful conjecture has resulted. It is more likely that the narrator used his own imagination here. The name Apama, borne by queens and other noble ladies, was familiar from Persia to Egypt, especially in the early 3d century B.C., the most probable date of the story. The king originally intended (and named) may have been Seleucus, or Ptolemy, or some other; but it is much more probable that it was Darius (III, Codomannus). This name would have been more likely to suggest to a Jewish reader the possibility of making use of the story. Also, the mention of Persia in 3:9, 14 seems to belong to the original text.

Another question relates to the possible adaptation of the story to its use in a Jewish history. One or two alterations for this purpose can be recognized with some probability. The verses 3:1, 2 describe Darius the Mede; close examination of chapters 3–5 has established this. There is a reference to Dan. 6:1 f., where "a hundred and twenty-*seven* satraps" seems to have been the original reading, see 6:1, 3 in the LXX.[48] The beginning of the story in its Gentile form may have been: "King Darius made a great feast for all his subjects and for all that were born in his house, and for the princes of Persia and all the satraps and captains and governors that were under him."

47. Observe that this editor, also, held the then orthodox view of the order of succession of the Medo-Persian rulers: Darius the Mede, Cyrus, Ahasuerus (the last king of the Perso-Median coalition), Artaxerxes I, Darius Nothus, etc.; the view held by the Chronicler, Daniel (both halves), and the interpolator of the story.

48. This part of Daniel was written at about the year 245 B.C., as the present writer demonstrated in 1909.

Another very probable improvement for Jewish use is to be seen in the *twofold* thesis of the third contestant (see above). The devout young Jewish guardsman (see 4:58 ff.) could hardly have been satisfied to leave the supreme power in the hands of women; nor would he endanger his case by antagonizing the king and his nobles. The interpolator solved the problem excellently by adding the praise of Truth, and including in it a casual mention of the one supreme God (4:35, 40 last clause).

The interpolation of the story must have taken place at an early date, before the Chronicler's work was well known; otherwise, this expanded form of the history would hardly have been allowed to supersede the other, even though its doctrine of Medo-Persian history was precisely that which was currently held.

The work of the "editor" who introduced Zerubbabel in 4:13, transposed the section Ezra 4:6–24, and made the slight alterations in 1 Esd. 5:2, 6, probably dates from the last century B.C.

Literature. See §9; also "The Story of the Three Youths," *Am. Jour. Sem. Langs., 23* (1907), 177–201, reprinted in *Ezra Studies.*

§12. THE ADDITIONS TO DANIEL

THE Additions to the book of Daniel, three in number, are regularly present in the manuscripts of the Greek Bible, and were included by Jerome in his Latin translation. The Biblical stories of Daniel were such popular favorites that they naturally received embellishment and expansion of various kinds.

One of the accretions is an insertion in the text of the canonical book, increasing the bulk of the third chapter by 67 verses. This consists mainly of a hymn sung by Daniel's three companions as they walked about in the blazing furnace. Preceding the hymn is a prayer uttered by Azariah, one of their number, and there are also a few connecting verses of narrative. The place where all this is inserted is between verses 23 and 24 of the Hebrew text.

The other Additions are popular tales illustrating Daniel's wisdom, but having no other connection with the canonical book. The story of Susanna stands in most Greek manuscripts at the beginning of the Daniel material, for the reason that the prophet is here represented as a mere youth. The stories of Bel and the Dragon occupy the last place in the group.

A. *The Prayer of Azariah and the Hymn of the Three Men*

In the Greek Daniel the two verses 3:24 f. are introductory; then follows the prayer, occupying verses 26–45. Azariah's long prayer is not for deliverance from the fire; it was too late for any such petition, and the three had already expressed their faith (vs. 17). He prays for his people, confessing their sin which has brought on them the present distress, and imploring pardon and mercy. As touching the immediate circumstances: "Let all those who afflict thy servants be confounded, and let them know that thou art the only God." If a prayer was to be uttered at this juncture, Azariah's is well suited to its place.

The Greek is very obviously the result of translation from Semitic. The original language was Hebrew, as Bennett (in Charles's *Apocrypha*) and others have contended. Such peculiarly Hebrew idioms as those in verses 34 and 40 are decisive.

The Hymn of the Three Men,[49] occupying verses 52–90, is a song of praise resembling Psalm 148 (much expanded) in its conception, and Psalm 136 in its constant repetition of a single refrain. Verse 88 gives the hymn connection with the scene in which it is located: Hananiah, Azariah, and Mishael are exhorted to praise the Lord, who has saved them from the flames of the furnace. The original language of the hymn was evidently Hebrew, like that of the prayer; and there appears no sufficient reason for doubting that both were written by the same hand, for this place.[50]

B. *Susanna*

This is a well-told story with a universally familiar motive, the narrow escape from death of an innocent victim, virtue triumphing over villainy. It illustrates the danger of a hasty verdict, and the possibility that wisdom divinely given to a youth, or even to a child, may reverse the judgment of grown men.

Susanna, the wife of a wealthy Israelite in Babylonia, is coveted by two elders of the people, who have been inflamed by her beauty. Driven by circumstances to mutual cónfession, they make common cause. Contriving to come upon her as she is bathing in her garden, they threaten her with disgrace and death if she does not yield herself to them. She

---

49. The title in the English version, "Song of the Three Holy Children," was obtained from the Greek, ὕμνος τῶν τριῶν παίδων, in which, however, the word παῖς represented Hebrew *'ebed*, "servant," as in Ps. 113 (112):1, etc.

50. Not necessarily for the place *in our canonical text* of the book. There must have been several "editions" of Daniel; and the shockingly awkward connection made in vs. 91a of the LXX looks like an attempt to fit in at this point the words of another version.

chooses the former alternative, and cries for help. The household servants and others rush in, and are told by the elders how they found her in the arms of a young man, who escaped. On the morrow there is a formal trial, and the two accusers, who are not only elders but also judges of the people, repeat their story. Susanna pleads not guilty, and calls God to witness. The two elders and judges, as men of high repute, are believed. Susanna is condemned to death and led away. The outcry of a youth (Daniel), charging false accusation, halts the procession, and the trial is renewed with Daniel as judge. He convicts the two of false witness, Susanna is vindicated, and the wicked elders are slain.

The story is one that might be told at any time, and in any land; it probably dates from the last century B.C. There is no reason for questioning its Jewish origin, for the Jews were as good story-tellers as their neighbors. Whether it was originally told of Daniel may indeed be doubted, for the concluding sentences of the "LXX" text, that of the single Chisian codex 87, speak of wisdom sometimes bestowed on "Israelite youth," with no mention here of Daniel.

Our standard Greek text of Daniel is that of Theodotion. At the time when he made his translation (after the middle of the 2d century A.D.), there were still Hebrew-Aramaic manuscripts of Daniel which included the additions. Theodotion's Greek of Susanna plainly suggests a Hebrew original, and it contains Hebrew idioms which are not Aramaic, see for example the middle of verse 15.[51] The famous third-century controversy over the original language has received mention in the General Introduction, see §6.

C. *Bel and the Dragon*

These are two separate but connected stories, of somewhat inferior quality, designed to ridicule idolatry; intended also to show Daniel's wisdom. The scene in each case is Babylon. In Theodotion's version the king is Cyrus;[52] in the Chisian (LXX) manuscript he is not named, but both texts declare Daniel to be a "companion" of the monarch.

Clear proof that the great statue of Bel is a living being is claimed to be given especially by the fact that he devours each night the huge amount of food and drink that is placed beside him. Daniel succeeds, by an obvious trick, in showing that the priests of the god are the real

51. The text of the unique "LXX" manuscript is defective, and its relation to Theodotion's text has not yet been made clear.

52. In the first verse the original reading was certainly *"Darius the son of* Astyages." At the conquest of Babylon, "Darius the Mede received the kingdom" (Dan. 6:1), and according to the early Jewish historians he was succeeded by his Persian partner Cyrus. He is the son of Astyages in Josephus, *Antt.,* 10, xi, 4.

consumers of the provisions. The king accordingly destroys Bel, and the priests are slain.

A monstrous dragon is worshiped in Babylon. Daniel, summoned to do homage to it, feeds it with a concoction of pitch, fat, and hair which causes it to burst asunder. The people, enraged by this treatment of their god, compel the king to have Daniel thrown into the den of lions. He remains there for six days, and the lions, though deprived of their customary food, do him no harm. On the sixth day, as Daniel, like the lions, feels the pangs of hunger, food is miraculously provided for him. The prophet Habakkuk, in the act of carrying food and drink to the reapers in a field in Judea, is arrested by an angel and borne by the hair of his head to the lions' den in Babylon, where he delivers the food to Daniel; then, in the twinkling of an eye, he is set down again in the field in Judea. On the seventh day, the king rescues Daniel from the den, and those who tried to destroy him are thrown to the lions.

According to the superscription in the Chisian manuscript, the stories of Bel and the Dragon were taken "from the prophecy of Habakkuk the son of Jeshua, of the tribe of Levi." Jewish legend indeed runs wild in its account of this prophet. He is declared to be the son of the Shunammite woman mentioned in 2 Kings 4:17–37, who in his boyhood was restored to life by Elisha, and yet is made a contemporary of Daniel. See also the story told in the *Lives of the Prophets*.

The Greek of Bel and the Dragon is of the translation variety. The original language was doubtless Hebrew, as in the case of the other additions to Daniel. The time when the stories were composed was presumably the last century B.C.

Literature. See §9; also Baumgartner, "Susanna, die Geschichte einer Legende," *Archiv für Religionswissenschaft, 24* (1926), 259–280; *27* (1929), 187 f.

§13. THE REST OF THE BOOK OF ESTHER

THE Greek Esther is a longer book than the Hebrew, containing all the material of the latter and much more. The portions found in the Greek but wanting in the Hebrew are the following:

1. Mordecai's dream; and the account of his foiling a conspiracy against the life of the king. This, a chapter of seventeen verses, precedes chapter 1 of the Hebrew. It is now generally designated as Section A. In our English Apocrypha this portion is numbered as xi, 2–xii, 6, following the enumeration of the Latin Bible (see below).

2. Section B. The copy of a letter sent out by the king, command-

ing the destruction of all the Jews in his kingdom. This follows 3:13 of the Hebrew. The Latin enumeration is xiii, 1–7.

3. Section C. The prayers of Mordecai and Esther. These follow chapter 4 of the Hebrew. In the Latin Bible Mordecai's prayer is numbered as xiii, 8–18, and Esther's as xiv, 1–19.

4. Section D. Esther's audience with the king; a narrative covering sixteen verses, where the Hebrew has only two (5:1 f.). In the Latin Bible this is xv, 1–16.

5. Section E. The copy of a letter sent out by the king, telling of Haman's end, praising the Jews, and permitting them to defend themselves against their enemies. This follows 8:12 of the Hebrew. The Latin enumeration, xvi, 1–24.

6. Section F. This includes two very diverse matters. The first of them is the interpretation of Mordecai's dream (see Section A), leading to a final word as to the significance of the feast of Purim. This follows the Hebrew Esther, and forms the close of the Greek version. In the Latin Bible, and hence in the English Apocrypha, it is numbered x, 4–13. The second part of the section is an important historical note appended to the Greek version. This is numbered xi, 1.

In the English Apocrypha, the bewildering sequence of these six unconnected portions of the Greek Esther is rendered especially chaotic by the fact that Section F with its colophon stands at the beginning, the interpretation of Mordecai's dream thus preceding the narration of the dream itself. The explanation of this is that Jerome, after finishing his Latin version of the Hebrew Esther, chapters 1:1–10:3, continued his translation with that of the Greek ending (including the colophon), and then proceeded with the other Greek portions in their proper order. Hence, in the Latin Bible, the succession of supplementary chapters from 10:4 to 16:24. The English version adopted the disorder which Jerome had created.

It has been customary to speak of these Greek sections as "additions" to Esther, but recent study has shown that the term needs qualification. The original Esther of the feast of Purim was the longer book, and our canonical Hebrew is a late abridgment, the "*second* letter of Purim" (9:29). See the *Harvard Theol. Rev., 37* (1944), 1–40. The original language of the story was Aramaic, and from this the Greek translation was made in Jerusalem, in the year 114 B.C., by an Egyptian scholar who is named. Sections A, C, D, and F (minus the colophon!) were all present in the text which was translated at that time. Sections B and E, obviously Greek compositions, were presumably the work of the translator just mentioned, their purpose being to increase, for the Egyptian readers, the impression of a true history.

Sections C and D, containing the prayers of Mordecai and Esther and the dramatic account of Esther's reception by the king, were necessarily left out of the book in the revision (2d century A.D.) which removed all religious formulas and every mention of God, at a time when the manner of observing the feast had become so hilarious, even boisterous, that there was danger of blasphemy.[53]

Sections A and F formed no part of the original story. They were an early accretion, however, and were present in the Aramaic version which was rendered into Greek in 114 B.C. If (as seems probable) they were in the Greek text which Josephus used, they were discarded by him as plainly secondary and disturbing.

The Aramaic Esther circulated in several forms, and more than one Greek translation was made. In addition to the standard Greek there has survived another text found in a few manuscripts, published in the editions of Fritzsche and Lagarde as well as in the Cambridge LXX, and commonly designated as Esther *alpha*. The variant readings thus gained are especially important in Sections C and D. In general, it is to the Greek, not to the Hebrew, that the reader must go in order to have the story of Mordecai and Esther in its true form and extent.

Literature. See §9; also Torrey, "The Older Book of Esther," *Harvard Theol. Rev., 37* (1944), 1–40. B. Jacob, "Das Buch Esther bei den LXX," *Zeitschr. f. d. alttest. Wissenschaft, 10* (1890), 241–298.

§14. BARUCH

BARUCH the son of Neriah, the companion and secretary of the prophet Jeremiah, had an important place in Jewish legend. Since it was taken for granted that he must have been an author as well as an amanuensis, certain anonymous writings already in existence were assigned to him, while others were freely composed in his name. Reputed to have been a witness of the last scenes of the downfall of the Judean kingdom, he would naturally be expected to write about the events of that time, as in the document now before us.

The book which bears his name is a composite work, of uneven quality. It consists of two distinct parts, unlike in character and of diverse authorship yet not incongruous, put together in order to make a book worthy of its reputed author. The first half, 1:1–3:8, is a composition in prose, definitely connected with Baruch; the second half, 3:9–5:9, is poetry, consisting of exhortations to Israel in captivity. The poetry

---

53. The Talmud, Megillah 7b, has this prescription for celebrating Purim: "Drink wine until you are no longer able to distinguish between 'cursed be Haman' and 'blessed be Mordecai.'" The official document of such a celebration must avoid the use of sacred names and phrases!

of this latter section, while made up largely of reminiscences of older works, especially Second Isaiah, is an impressive composition written with evident feeling and with no little skill. It is a plausible conjecture that these anonymous pictures of Israel in exile first gave to some one the suggestion of a book of Baruch, and that the first half of the present work was composed as an introduction to the typical "prophecy" in metric form. It is throughout well suited to this purpose, and the prayer of which it chiefly consists is given close connection, in 3:8, with the poem which begins at 3:9. "The words of the book which Baruch wrote" (1:1), accordingly, are the entire composition, both prayer and psalm, 1:15–5:9. This is the book that was to be read to the people assembled in the temple at Jerusalem on the several festal days (1:14).

The book professes to have been written in Babylon (1:1), at a date concerning which there has been much controversy. The present text reads (1:2): "in the fifth year, on the seventh day of the month, at the time when the Chaldeans took Jerusalem and burned it with fire." In view of what follows almost immediately in the document, verses 6 f., 10, and 14, it seems clear (to the present writer) that the closing words of the date are a conventional formula loosely used, meaning simply, "at the time when Jerusalem was captured and destroyed," covering the whole period from the deportation under Jehoiachin to the end of Zedekiah's reign. The author of these words of Baruch certainly knew that when the Chaldeans took the city the second time *they burned the temple*, but in the present book there is no indication of any impairment of the regular service; we read of burnt offerings, sin offerings, incense, oblations upon the altar, and of assemblies "in the house of the Lord" on the usual festal occasions.[54]

The date "the fifth year," in 1:2, can only be the fifth year of the reign of Zedekiah (or of the captivity of Jehoiachin), see verse 3. So many students of the book have held. The number of the month is missing, probably by accident.

The presence of Baruch in Babylonia at this time is not necessarily incongruous with what is told of him in Jer. 43:6 f., namely, that after the murder of Gedaliah (2 Kings 25:25) he was carried to Egypt along with Jeremiah. There are however several conflicting stories in regard to this prophet's last years and the place of his death, no one of the legends having any especial claim to superiority. It has sometimes been conjectured (see Gifford, in Wace's *Apocrypha*, p. 247)

---

54. The one apparent exception, in 2:26, is not such in reality, for the allusion to "the house laid waste" is merely copied from the prayer in the book of Daniel which is borrowed here (see below). The passage in Daniel is 9:17, and the concluding words of the verse (see the LXX!) are also taken over in Baruch.

that Baruch himself was to be the bearer of the message and the contribution sent at this time to the people in Jerusalem, including his
book and "the silver vessels which Zedekiah had made." Why this purpose, if it existed, should have been concealed in our narrative is not
apparent. It is plainly implied in 1:14 that the book is *not* to be
brought to Jerusalem by its author, nor is it to be read there publicly
by him, but by the priests.[55]

The bulk of the first half of the book consists of a prayer borrowed
from the ninth chapter of Daniel, quoted often verbally, but greatly
expanded so that it extends over some fifty verses. There is first a
confession of sins, 1:15–2:10; then the petition for forgiveness and
mercy, 2:11–3:8. The language is largely a mosaic of familiar phrases,
and there are considerable quotations, more or less altered, from
Isaiah, Leviticus, Deuteronomy, and Jeremiah (see especially 2:21–
25); nevertheless the whole composition is effective for its purpose and
suited to the place which it occupies. The scene of the public reading
in Babylonia is obtained from Ezra 8:15, 21, 31, for "the river Sud"
is none other than the river Ahava of the earlier narrative.[56]

The second half of the book—the older portion, originally anonymous, which was claimed for Baruch—begins with a didactic passage
in metric form which has for its subject "the fountain of wisdom."
Israel has forsaken this fountain, and for this reason is in exile, "waxen
old [57] in a strange country." The true wisdom is hid from the world,
the sages of the earth have not found her. Her ways cannot be searched
out. (Here the writer makes use of Job, chaps. 28 and 38.) God gave
her to Israel; she appeared on earth and moved among men (3:38).
She is embodied in the law, the book of the commandments of God
(4:1).[58] Here, in the God-given wisdom, Israel will find light and life.

At this point, 4:5, the author of the poem strikes another key and
begins a song of comfort and encouragement. The transition to the
new theme and to a formally distinct division of his composition is both
typical and effective. The connection with the preceding division is
perfect, see verses 4 and 5, while the meter now changes from the

55. The curious vs. 1:8, with its silver vessels to be carried back to Judea(!), has
rightly been pronounced an interpolation; the author of the book would at least have
given it a plausible connection with its context. Some one who wished to see Baruch
return to Jerusalem undertook this improvement, perhaps originally in the form of a
marginal note.

56. It has already been shown by J. A. Bewer, *Jour. Bib. Lit., 43,* 226 f., that mere
corruption of an uncial Greek text has produced the new name, ΕΟΥΑ (Ahava) being
read as ΣΟΥΔ.

57. This is plainly not the time of Baruch. The writer thinks rather of the exile as
near its end; so also in the second division of the poem, which begins at 4:5.

58. It is unfortunate that a chapter division(!) should have been made at this point.
The result is to obscure the meaning of both verses, before and after the false division.

didactic 3|3 to the lyric 3|2, as Harwell has shown (see the reference, below).

The prophet, speaking in the name of Yahweh, at first addresses Israel in a tone that is partly reproachful, partly reassuring (4:5–9a).[59] Then Jerusalem, personified, takes the word in a dramatic passage (vss. 9b–29) which resembles Is. 49:14–21; 51:17–23; 54:1–17, and the book of Lamentations. The woes pronounced on Babylon in verses 25, 32–35, destruction, desolation, fire, and "demons," merely repeat the familiar prophecies in Is. 34:14, 13:21 f., Jer. 50:39, and Is. 47:9, 11, 14. From this point on to the end (4:30–5:9), Jerusalem is no longer the speaker but is addressed, and there is only encouragement and splendid promise, with Second Isaiah as the model.

It has in recent years been a widely accepted view that the section 4:36–5:9 shows dependence on the eleventh of the Psalms of Solomon, for the verbal coincidences in the Greek are both numerous and striking. Since it was believed that the original language of this portion of Baruch was Greek and that it was composed after 70 A.D.(!), while the date of the Psalms of Solomon is the middle of the last century B.C., the question of the order of dependence seemed to be settled. In fact, however, the original language of Baruch was Hebrew throughout, and the entire book was rendered into Greek hardly later than the middle of the 2d century B.C. As to this, see below. If the agreement between the Greek of Baruch and that of the eleventh of the Psalms of Solomon proves dependence, then the latter work is the borrower.

This "book of Baruch" is in its entirety a work of unusual interest, but the elaborate poem 3:9–5:9, which is its main constituent, is especially important and deserving of more attention than it has generally received in modern times. As the last dying flame of typical Hebrew *prophecy*, in the literature known to us, it has a unique place among the apocryphal books. It is written in frank imitation of the older models, and yet has its own good measure of originality. It is a poem well conceived and constructed, often eloquent in its expression, and the feeling is unmistakably genuine and deep throughout. In short, we have here an impressive utterance of Israelite penitence, distress, and triumphant faith, suggesting in its every portion the atmosphere of the latest canonical prophecies.

The original language in both halves of the book was Hebrew. This has almost universally been held to be true for the first half, and

59. In the very first line (4:5) there was a false reading in the Hebrew text which the Greek translator rendered, *zikrōn* instead of *zikrū*. The correct rendering is: "Be of good cheer, my people; *remember,* O Israel!" It is the same exhortation which Second Isaiah gives in 44:21, 46:8 and 9; compare also 51:1–4. Here in Baruch the prophet proceeds, in vs. 8: "You have *forgotten* the everlasting God who brought you up."

Kneucker and Harwell, especially, have shown it to be the case also in the second half. Indeed, the translation-Greek here is unmistakable, even without the decisive proof furnished by such examples as the one given in the footnote above.

The Greek rendering of the book was the work of a single translator; see H. St. John Thackeray, *The Septuagint and Jewish Worship* (1921), p. 87. It was this same translator, moreover, who rendered the second half of Jeremiah into the Greek of our LXX (there was a division of labor here, as in the translation of one or two others of the longer books); see especially Thackeray, *Grammar of the Old Testament in Greek* (1909), p. 12.[60] This should surprise no one, since the book bears Baruch's name, and in all the Greek usage known to us, including the Jewish (see the General Introduction, in several places), it is treated as though it were a part of Jeremiah. Now the Greek version of Jeremiah is attested by the Sirach prologue as existing in Egypt in 132 B.C., for Bar Sira's grandson appeals incidentally to the evidence afforded by the Greek renderings of "the Prophets and the rest of the books"; see Swete's *Introduction to the Old Testament in Greek*, p. 24; also *The Second Isaiah*, p. 102. The Greek translation of the entire book of Baruch, then, was in existence at this date.

The Hebrew original of the first half of the book, 1:1–3:8, was written at some time subsequent to the year 164 B.C., as follows from its unquestioned dependence on the book of Daniel, not only in the prayer based on chapter 9 but also in the references to Belshazzar (Baltasar) the son of Nebuchadnezzar (as in Daniel, chap. 5). As was remarked above, this half of Baruch seems to have been composed as an introduction to the older poetical composition. Is there any other plausible way of explaining it? Taken by itself it gets nowhere, and there are no "words of Baruch" excepting the borrowed and expanded prayer, which could fairly be termed *mere* padding if it were less eloquent and heartfelt. It would not have been a happy thought to send to the people of Jerusalem, for public reading, this depressing little document ending with such a verse as 3:8; they were able to do their own wailing. What they needed was encouragement. But the real purpose of the composition was well served; in spite of its historical weaknesses, which every commentator exposes, it is a very respectable prologue to the prophecy which it aimed to preserve.

The date of the Hebrew prophecy itself, 3:9–5:9, can only be conjectured within rather wide limits. On the one hand, it is later than

60. Nevertheless Thackeray, because of his belief that the second half of Baruch is a very late work brought forth by the catastrophe of A.D. 70, is forced to question in his later book (mentioned above), p. 87, what he had previously declared to be "beyond a doubt."

Job (4th century?) ; on the other hand, it is a composition which has its only analogies in the canonical Hebrew scriptures. A date somewhere in the third century seems the best conjecture. The circumstances in which the Jews then found themselves—the chosen people scattered abroad, Judah and Jerusalem in seemingly more hopeless subjection than at any previous time, completely in the power of a more vicious "beast" than the bear or the leopard (Dan. 7:7), with the prediction of Deut. 28:49 f. (Baruch 4:15) now fully realized— these circumstances might well have led a writer of imagination to take up again the well-worn theme, the "captivity" of Israel, giving the familiar pictures and phrases a new application. This, exactly, is what we see before us.

The Hebrew text of the book perished at the end of the 1st century A.D. (see the General Introduction), and our only knowledge of it is derived, directly or indirectly, from the Greek version.

Literature. See §9; also J. J. Kneucker, *Das Buch Baruch* (Leipzig, 1879), a very thorough work. R. R. Harwell, *The Principal Versions of Baruch* (Yale dissertation, 1915). H. St. J. Thackeray, *The Septuagint and Jewish Worship* (Schweich Lectures, 1923).

§15. The Epistle of Jeremiah

In the book of Jeremiah there is a curious passage which has always aroused interest and given rise to speculation. The 52 chapters of the prophecy are all written in good Hebrew, but the single verse 10:11 is Aramaic. Why? The query has had no satisfactory answer. The verse reads: *Thus shall ye say unto them, The gods that have not made the heavens and the earth, they shall perish from the earth and from under these heavens.* The second person plural, *"ye* shall say unto them," evidently refers to men of Israel who are now commanded to give this message to the Gentiles.

The Epistle of Jeremiah is concerned solely with the folly of idol worship. Its opening words—properly the superscription of the letter —are these: "A copy of the letter which Jeremiah sent to those who were about to be led captive to Babylon by the king of the Babylonians, to instruct them, as he had been commanded by God." Here is a situation similar to that which is implied in the verse of the prophecy, quoted above, but not necessarily the same situation. The relation of the Epistle to the tenth chapter of Jeremiah is very close. There are plain reminiscences of Jer. 10:3–5, 8 f., and 14 f.; and the words "fear them not" from verse 5 of the prophecy occur again and again in the

Epistle, as a sort of refrain. The prophet is elsewhere (Jer. 29) represented as writing to the exiles in Babylonia, though with instruction of quite another nature. It was easy now to imagine (and compose) a letter directly suggested by the Aramaic verse 10:11.

The Epistle is long drawn out, covering 72 verses, not counting the superscription, which belonged to the original document. It is a formless composition, rambling and repetitious, from the literary point of view decidedly inferior, and with not many items of interest. Ridicule of the Gentile gods was not uncommon in the later Hebrew literature, beginning with the ironical poetry of Is. 44:9–20, and continued especially in Psalms 115 and 135. The writer of the Epistle enlarges on the old models with an exuberant imagination. The wooden deity becomes a roost for bats, swallows, various birds, "and even cats" (vs. 22). The food offered to the idol is not only sold or devoured by the priests, but their wives also salt down some of it (vs. 28). A crutch[61] that has proved its strength, or a household utensil that is serviceable, is better than a Gentile god (vs. 59). Any one of these deities is as useless "as a scarecrow in a cucumber field" (vs. 70).

The closing words of the letter (vs. 73), drawing the conclusion from its teaching, should perhaps be rendered: "The Jew, then, is better off without any images, for he will be far from reproach." There was a time when the adjective "just, righteous," was used in a suitable context as a synonym for "Israelite." This is clearly the case in the Greek Esther, 1:5, 6; and in the book of Wisdom, 18:7, there is a similar contrast between the Israelites and their Egyptian enemies, as also in verse 20. For a criticism of the usual rendering of the verse, see C. J. Ball, in Charles's *Apocrypha.*

As to the original language of the Epistle, the practically unanimous verdict of scholars has been, until recently, that expressed by Fritzsche in his commentary, I, 206: "If any one of the Apocryphal books was composed in Greek, this certainly was." Ball, in the work just cited, offered and defended the thesis of a Hebrew original, and presented a conjectural restoration of a large part of the text. The demonstration is unconvincing, however. It would be necessary to suppose that the original text had undergone very extensive corruption before the Greek translation was made. Aside from this, not one of the items of proof offered on pages 597 f. can be accepted as valid. If the examination by a scholar of Ball's thoroughness and wide learning can produce nothing better than this, it can be said with little hesitation that the language was probably *not* Hebrew.

61. Reading *pelek* instead of *melek,* "king," which makes no sense here. The word is both Hebrew and Aramaic, and has several meanings. For the meaning "crutch" see 2 Sam. 3:29 and the lexicons.

To any one who is well versed in the Greek of translation it must be clear that our text is the rendering of a Semitic original. Aramaic is then the obvious probability, even without the suggestion given by the strange verse in Jeremiah 10. There are in the Greek text several indications pointing in this direction, the most significant of them being the verse 10a (Engl. 11a). The author of the letter has just mentioned the gold and silver with which the images are overlaid, and has said that the priests sometimes take it, to enrich themselves. Verse 10 (11) adds: And some of it they will even "give to *the harlots on the roof*" (Ball's rendering; the only rendering that deals fairly with the Greek text). This "roof" has made trouble for all interpreters, both the ancient and the modern. The old translators were perplexed by it, obviously so; modern translators gain a half-satisfying result by discarding the Greek preposition and supposing a rare Greek word. Ball thinks that the harlots were on the roof "perhaps for coolness"; the priests, however, might have preferred a less conspicuous place.

It is a natural conjecture that the author meant to say that the gold was given to the harlots "for (their) hire," '*al agrā*, instead of "on the roof," '*al iggārā* (the same consonants). This is the "hire of a harlot," *agar zānīthā*, of Targ. Deut. 23:19 (18), doubtless the passage that suggested this item to the author of the Epistle. A clearer bit of evidence for Aramaic as the original language could hardly be desired.

At two points there are phrases which have interesting parallels in the New Testament. The "rust and decay (βρωμάτων, '*uklā*)" in verse 12 reminds of the "moth and decay (βρῶσις, '*uklā*)" of Matt. 6:19. In verse 71, the "purple and fine linen" intended by the author has become "purple and marble(!)" by the same mistranslation (demonstrated by Ball) which is found in Rev. 15:6. See my *Documents of the Primitive Church*, p. 213. The Hebrew-Aramaic *šēš*, *šaiš*, representing two very different words, continued to be used in Palestine in both meanings, "linen" and "marble"; while in Egypt, apparently, at the time when this translation was made the Aramaic word was known only in the latter signification.

For the time of composition of the Epistle, a date near the beginning of the 2d century B.C. seems most probable. In the Greek Bible it was regularly treated as an appendage to the book of Jeremiah; thus always by the early Christians (see the General Introduction), and apparently at first by the Egyptian Jews. There is also an item of more definite evidence, which has not hitherto been seen in its true importance. In 2 Macc. 2:1 f. we are told of instruction given by the prophet Jeremiah *to those who were about to be led captive to Babylonia*. Included in this is the warning to them, "not to be led astray in their minds when they should see images of gold and silver, and the adornment upon them." This is certainly a reference to our Epistle. The passage in Second Maccabees is in an Aramaic letter sent by the authorities in Jerusalem to the Jews of Egypt in the year 124 B.C.; and the fact thus appears that the Epistle, in its original Aramaic form, was held in importance by the Jews of Palestine.

Hence, it may be conjectured, the strange *Aramaic* verse (10:11) in the book of Jeremiah. The verse was originally Hebrew, but the change to Aramaic was authorized after the publication of the Epistle, in order to give to the latter a certain presumption of authenticity. This added new interest both to the letter and to Jeremiah's prophecy.

The Targum of Jer. 10:11 (the Aramaic verse) makes reference to *a letter* of Jeremiah warning the Babylonian exiles against the idols which they would see in the new surroundings; and the question has been debated, whether this is not a direct reference to the Epistle. The answer should be negative. The targumist certainly knew of our Epistle and was interested in it, but he had no intention of referring to it, since it had finally been rejected by the authorities. He merely gives an expanded paraphrase of the Aramaic verse, and declares the above-mentioned letter to have been addressed to "the residue of the elders of the Babylonian captivity," that is, *to the recipients of the letter given in Jeremiah 29.* Whether he actually knew of any such letter of the prophet may be strongly doubted.

In the Latin Vulgate, and consequently in our English Bible, the Epistle is attached to Baruch, as its sixth chapter. In the Greek manuscripts it has no fixed position, though always included in the Jeremiah group.

Literature. See §9; also H. St. J. Thackeray, *Some Aspects of the Greek Old Testament* (1927), pp. 53–64.

§16. The Prayer of Manasseh

"The Lord is merciful and gracious, slow to anger, and abundant in lovingkindness. He will not always chide, neither will he keep his anger forever" (Ps. 103:8 f.). It was conviction of this, and the wish to give it signal illustration, that brought forth the prayer which is included in some lists of the Jewish Apocrypha. King Manasseh's sin, in abandoning the Mosaic law and introducing foreign cults, as described in Second Kings 21 and mirrored in the prophecy of Ezekiel, was unique in its dire result: it brought upon Judah the destruction of Jerusalem and the temple, and the Babylonian captivity (2 Kings 23:36 f., 24:3 f., Jer. 15:4). "Yahweh would not pardon" (24:4). In Second

Chronicles, however, the sin which could not be pardoned is transferred entire from Manasseh to Zedekiah (36:14 ff.), while the former king is declared to have repented, and to have restored the true worship; and to have uttered a prayer which was preserved in writing (33:11–19).

Whatever may be conjectured as to the existence of such a prayer in the Chronicler's time, the example known to us can hardly claim so early a date. No Jewish writer subsequent to the Chronicler shows knowledge of any such document. In its Greek form, it is all but unknown to the LXX manuscripts; and when it does appear in them, it is not in connection with Chronicles, but in a collection of hymns and odes appended to the Psalter; thus in the Alexandrinus and in the Zurich Psalter (Codex T), also in the manuscripts of the Ethiopic version. It was not in Origen's Bible, nor is it ever mentioned by Jerome, who apparently had no knowledge of its existence. As was said above, in the General Introduction, the prayer seems to have had no early Latin translation, and in the Vulgate manuscripts it appears only at a late date.[62] The Greek is first attested by the Syriac *Didascalia*, a work of the 3d century translated from the Greek. The prayer is here appended to the Chronicler's account of Manasseh's repentance. The Greek text itself first appears in the *Apostolical Constitutions*, II, 22; this being a work of the 4th century which incorporates the *Didascalia*.

The author of the prayer, however, was certainly not a Christian, but a Jew. No sure ground has been seen for a conjecture as to the date of its composition. It is not found in any early list of the Jewish "outside books," and thus to all appearance it is an intruder in the group, as was said in the General Introduction. For this reason it has commonly been regarded by scholars as of late date, perhaps even of the second or third century of the present era. The belief that its original language was Greek, added to the fact of its late appearance, made the decision most natural.

The verdict needs to be revised, however. The original language of the prayer was not Greek, but Hebrew. Even in this very brief portion of text the evidence of translation is more than once clear and decisive. The curious Greek of verse 4 represents a Semitic original whose rendering should be: (Thou,) "before whose power all things shudder and tremble." [63] Equally evident is the true reading of verse 5b: "Insupportable is the burning of thine anger at sinners"; where two Hebrew words are rendered in the Greek conventionally, and here

62. In the earlier editions of the Vulgate—earlier than the Council of Trent—the prayer is placed after Second Chronicles.

63. R. H. Charles, *Apocrypha and Pseudepigrapha of the Old Testament*, I, 615, footnote, had seen this.

wrongly. Verse 10a should have been rendered: "I am bowed down with many iron bands so that I cannot lift up my head, *if I have not forgiveness*" (see vs. 13!); the Greek corresponds exactly to this Hebrew. These examples may suffice. C. J. Ball, in Wace's *Apocrypha*, II, 361–371, inclined to believe the Greek a translation, but could find no direct evidence of this.

The question of the date is thus given a new turn. The Christians of the 2d or 3d century found the prayer where they had found the rest of the apocrypha, in Egypt, and in Greek translation. It may have been there in Jewish hands, unnoticed, for a very long time. As Fritzsche, *Handbuch*, I, 158, remarks, such a little document, preserved by itself, not in connection with any Biblical book, would not easily have attracted notice or have been given mention. To the Jews, it was a *curiosum* of no great interest. One of their learned men, in the last century B.C. or the 1st century A.D., had undertaken to compose such a prayer as the book of Chronicles mentioned, and the achievement proved him equal to the task. It is a composition well conceived and expressed, and in every way worthy to hold its place among the apocrypha. If its original Hebrew form could be restored, it would be found to be couched in true metric form throughout. The Greek text is printed in Fritzsche's *Libri Apocryphi Vet. Test.*, pp. 92 f., and in Swete's *Old Testament in Greek*, III, 824–826.

Literature. See §9.

§17. First Maccabees

The "Maccabees," sons of Mattathias of Modin, were the leaders of the Jewish patriots in their struggle against Antiochus Epiphanes and his immediate successors. Originally, the name belonged to only one of the sons, Judas (Maccabeus),[64] the outstanding figure in the uprising. The First and Second books of Maccabees are histories of the struggle. Third Maccabees, dealing with events of another time, received its unsuitable name merely as an account of the persecution of Jews by a king, and their triumph. Fourth Maccabees is a philosophical treatise which takes its chief illustration from the steadfastness of certain famous Maccabean martyrs, hence the title.

64. The origin of the name is obscure. The time-honored explanation as "the hammerer" is questionable for more than one reason, but especially because the supposed weapon is not the sledge-hammer, *paṭṭish,* of Jer. 23:29, 50:23(!), and Is. 41:7, but the smaller, workman's tool.

First Maccabees is a work of high quality, whether viewed as history or as literature. It was composed in Hebrew; but in this case also, as in that of all the other outside books written in Hebrew or Aramaic, the original language was not preserved. How the book was originally entitled is not known.[65] It is a concise account of Jewish affairs, chiefly military and political, from the uprising at Modin in 167 B.C. to the murder of the prince and high priest Simon in 134.

A brief introductory paragraph (1:1–9) begins with the conquest of Alexander and describes in general terms the origin of the Seleucid empire. The conclusion of the first verse is generally mistranslated; read . . . "he reigned in his stead, as the first ruler of the Greek (i.e., Asiatic) empire."; cf. 6:2. The remainder of the first chapter, also introductory, pictures the desperate condition of the Jews of Palestine under Antiochus Epiphanes. The second chapter tells of the uprising at Modin and the growth of the rebellion led by Mattathias the Hasmonean. His five sons are named (the Greek form sometimes of uncertain origin): Gaddi, Thassi, Maqqabi, Hauran, Happus; these homely names replaced by famous Hebrew names, Johanan, Simeon, Judah, Eleazar, Jonathan, when the five brothers became national heroes.

The narrative here is twice interrupted, in true Semitic manner, by poetical interludes in Hebrew metric form. The first of these, verses 7–13, is Mattathias' lament over the desecration of Jerusalem and the persecution of the faithful people; the other, verses 49–68, is his exhortation to his sons at the end of his life. There are similar lyrical passages in other parts of the book.

With chapter 3 begins the story of the famous war for religious freedom and independence. The thrilling narrative of the first victories gained by the Jews under the leadership of Judas Maccabeus is followed by the account of the purification of the temple and dedication of the new altar, in the year 164. The course of the subsequent history while Judas was in command runs as follows. Campaigns against the surrounding nations (chap. 5). Death of Antiochus Epiphanes in Persia, and accession of Antiochus V Eupator, year 163. Further wars with the Syrians. Concession to the Jews of religious freedom, in return for their submission (all this in chap. 6). Demetrius Soter gains possession of the Seleucid throne. Defeat and death of Nicanor, the arch-enemy of the Jews, year 160. The day of this triumph, the thirteenth of Adar, set apart for a yearly celebration (these things in chap. 7). Treaty with the Romans; substance of the Romans' reply

65. The Aramaic title, "Book of the Hasmonean House," recorded by Origen and quoted from him by Eusebius, *H. E.* VI, 25, was presumably that of an Aramaic version made from the Greek early in the present era.

given in 8:23–32. Further warfare, 9:1–22; death of Judas in battle, year 160.

Jonathan succeeds Judas as military leader of the Jews. There follows a period of distress. John, one of the five sons of Mattathias, is treacherously seized and slain by a clan of Nabateans, who however soon pay for their deed. Notice the metrical verse of triumph, 9:41. Jonathan and Simon, after several reverses, gain the upper hand over the Syrians, and the war ends (9:73).

A pretender to the throne, Alexander Balas, now appears. Both he and Demetrius sue for the help of Jonathan, who makes good use of his opportunity. Supported by Alexander, he becomes the recognized high priest of the nation, year 152. In the ensuing battle of the two rivals Demetrius Soter is slain. Alexander makes an alliance with Ptolemy Philometor, king of Egypt, and the two kings receive Jonathan in state at Ptolemais (10:59–66).

Demetrius II Nicator, the son of D. Soter, arrives from Crete, gathers an army and challenges the Jews, sending against them Apollonius, one of his generals. In the campaigns which follow, Jonathan and Simon are able to hold their ground. Ptolemy now breaks faith with Alexander, enters Syria as conqueror, and transfers his alliance to Demetrius; Alexander is slain (11:1–19). Demetrius, now in undisputed possession of the Seleucid throne, enters into negotiations with Jonathan, who gains some important advantages. The king is disliked by his armies and by the people. He seeks Jonathan's aid, and in an insurrection at Antioch the king's life is saved by the Jewish soldiers; nevertheless he deals treacherously with the Jews (11:20–53).

A new claimant to the throne is brought forward at this favorable juncture, the boy Antiochus VI, whose regent, Tryphon, undertakes to rule. The disaffected Syrian armies flock to his side. Demetrius is compelled to flee, but is still able to harass the Jews, and Jonathan has a narrow escape (11:54–74). Jonathan sends ambassadors to Rome to renew the former treaty, and to the Spartans to reaffirm friendship and confederacy (12:1–23). The wall of Jerusalem is strengthened, and Simon adds to the fortresses of Judea (12:24–38). Tryphon gets possession of Jonathan by treachery, holds him as a hostage, and eventually puts him to death, end of the year 142 (12:39–53).

Simon, now the leader of the Jews, defies Tryphon (who has killed the boy Antiochus and put on the diadem) and demands concessions of Demetrius. The Jews secure political independence, year 141; see 13:41 f. The citadel in Jerusalem is rid of its Syrian garrison, and an annual festival is declared (chap. 13). The land enjoys a time of peace and prosperity. There is a renewal of friendly relations with the Spartans and with Rome. A formal record in honor of Simon is drawn up by the people and put in a conspicuous place; the text of the document is given in 14:27–47; this was in the year 140.

At about this time the king Demetrius was captured and held in captivity in Persia (14:1–3). His brother soon usurps the throne as Antiochus VII Sidetes. He at first confirms to Simon all that the Jews had gained, then enters Syria with an army and drives Tryphon out of the land. Turning now against the Jews he makes demands on them, and sends one of his generals against Judea (chap. 15). Simon's son John, to whom he had given the chief military command (13:53), defeats the Syrians. Simon and two of his sons are entrapped and murdered near Jericho; John, who was at Gazara, escapes (chap. 16).

It is evident from the foregoing synopsis that the author of First Maccabees was a true historian. It also seems clear that he was one who stood near to the center of Jewish political affairs. If his book was put forth at about the year 125 (see below), we may suppose that the uprising at Modin took place in his early manhood, that he had personal knowledge of much of the history which he records, and also unusual opportunities of gaining information. It can hardly be doubted that he lived and wrote in Palestine, and that his own interests were all in that land. His acquaintance with the geography and topography of the country is minute, and in his narrative he frequently introduces details which would have no importance for one living at a distance from the scenes and events described; see 3:24; 7:19; 9:2–4, 33 f., 43; 12:36 f.; 13:22 f.; 16:5 f. Throughout the book he shows himself to be a narrator of unusual ability, a scholar, and a man of rank and experience. He writes objectively and with restraint, only rarely throwing in a brief reflection of his own, as in 9:41, 11:53, and 16:17.

He is a stanch adherent of the Hasmoneans, the family divinely appointed to save Israel, as he implies in 5:62. He does not, indeed, employ here any word indicating divine choice, for it is a striking peculiarity of this history that it avoids every direct designation of God, using circumlocutions instead; a good example is the verse 16:3. The author is nevertheless a devout Israelite, zealous for the law and the ordinances, for the holy scriptures, and for Jerusalem and the sanctuary. The successes achieved by the Maccabean leaders are ascribed to the divine help in 4:55, 12:15, and elsewhere. The day of prophets and miracles is past (9:27), but "heaven" will still hear and answer prayer (3:18, 19, 44; 4:30–33, and often). See also 11:71 f.

On the ground of the closing words of the book, 16:23 f., "Now the rest of the acts of John, . . . behold, they are written in the chronicles of his high priesthood," etc., it has commonly been conjectured that its author put it forth after the death of Simon's famous son. If however the picture of the author given here is substantially correct, the date thus supposed for the publication of his book is impossible. The reign of John Hyrcanus (134–103) was glorious, renowned in subsequent years as one of Israel's great days. But all that the author of First Maccabees, worshipper of the Hasmonean princes, can say about him is that he waged war and did deeds (we knew this much from the preceding history) and "built the walls"; that is, rebuilt at about the year 127 the part that had been razed by Antiochus Sidetes. The writer of our history appears to think of John simply as the very promising son of Simon, and this can only mean that the deeds which brought Hyrcanus his chief renown were not yet done. First Maccabees must have been finished in the early part of his reign, probably about the year 125. Every feature of the book supports this supposition.[66]

As for the mention of "the rest of the acts," etc., this is merely a stock phrase borrowed from the Hebrew Bible, the most convenient way of ending the account of a great man. It neither informs us that there were other acts worthy of special mention, nor that a chronicle actually existed; it is only a complimentary flourish. This author varies it also in 9:22, in concluding the story of Judas; another writer makes use of it in Esther 10:2, in extolling the greatness of Ahasuerus. See further the *Encyclopaedia Biblica*, Vol. III, "First Maccabees," §5; also the *Harvard Theol. Rev.*, *37* (1944), 30 f.

The high quality of First Maccabees as a historical work has been generally recognized. The picture of this important period in Jewish history is by far the best that we have, and for much of it we have no other account; the dates given (according to the Seleucid era)[67] are trustworthy; the many interesting details make the impression of truth, and are confirmed wherever any other sources happen to be available. The strong Jewish bias can be taken for granted and is not disturbing. The author makes only brief mention of the defeats suffered by the Jewish armies, but it would not have occurred to him to change a defeat into a victory, as is done, for example, in 2 Macc. 13:9–24 (contrast 1 Macc. 6:28–63). His numerical estimates (size of armies, number of the slain, etc.) are of course mere guesses, not to be taken seriously. It is inevitable that there should be some other mistakes, in matters of fact or in the precise order of events. Second Maccabees is another history in which the story of this fight for religious freedom is largely based on personal recollection and oral information.

---

66. It is instructive to compare Enoch 90:9, in the famous vision of Israelite history, when John Hyrcanus is the "great horn." See § 27.

67. See the important investigation by Kolbe, *Beiträge zur syrischen und jüdischen Geschichte* (1926).

The two histories do not always agree, and neither of the two is always right.

Whatever written material was utilized in the book must have consisted of miscellaneous documents collected and freely used by the author. Style and method are remarkably uniform throughout the history, as is manifest even in the Greek, and there is nowhere evidence, nor likelihood, of a continuous written source. (Those who believe the book to have been written in the last century B.C. *must* postulate such sources.) This seems rather to be the account of one who had himself witnessed the whole Maccabean struggle from its beginning, and had acquaintances who had taken an active part in this or that phase of the mighty contest. There are in all portions of the history details which no one but a contemporary of the events would have recorded, such as 6:39 f., 7:33 ff., 8:19 (the "long journey" of the ambassadors to Rome), 9:34, 43 (where "on the sabbath day" has no significance for the narrative), 13:21 f., etc.

Where First Maccabees and Second Maccabees present the same picture of events over a series of years, it has seemed to some interpreters to mean that First Maccabees made use of the work of Jason of Cyrene, whose history is abridged by Second Maccabees. The explanation would rather seem to be this, that in these cases both histories give a true account; there is no evidence of literary dependence. Jason's work, put forth probably at about the same time as First Maccabees (see the following Section), was also a history based largely on oral information.

First Maccabees contains numerous letters, treaties, and other official documents, such as would be expected in a formal history. These, some or all, have by various scholars been pronounced interpolations. Also, chapters 14–16 have been very widely regarded as a later addition to the book; the reason for the strange opinion being found in the treatment of this history by Josephus. In his *Antiquities* he follows First Maccabees closely up to, and including, chapter 13; thereafter he makes no use of the book. Other evidence of the supposed editorial expansion is found in the account of Numenius and the golden shield, 1 Macc. 14:24; 15:15 ff. Josephus records this, but under similar circumstances at a later day.

The case against First Maccabees seemed strong, and at the close of the 19th century few voices were raised in defense of the disputed portions of the book,[68] but in recent years there has been increasing recognition of their genuineness. If literary style and individual traits count for anything, the author of 14–16 is identical with the author of 1–13.

68. See however the article "First Maccabees" in the *Encyclopaedia Biblica*.

The various official documents were given by him in free reproduction for substance, and to that extent they are trustworthy, for he certainly was well informed, and he plainly had the intention of making his history a true account. At more than one point important confirmation has come to light. The most thorough and convincing defense of the book as it stands before us is H. W. Ettelson's *The Integrity of I Maccabees. Transactions of the Connecticut Academy of Arts and Sciences, 27* (1925), 249–384. This demonstration, which in briefer form was submitted as a dissertation for the Ph.D. degree at Yale University in 1915, is conclusive against those who hold that First Maccabees received an addendum, and gives strong reasons for believing that the incorporated documents are more valuable than modern commentators generally have supposed.

Ettelson's argument finds principal support in the fact, already quite generally acknowledged and now considerably reinforced by him, that Josephus used the book in its Greek form, and that he had before him the very same (corrupt) text which we have. There follows a clear presentation of the evidence that all parts of the book, including the supposed addendum and the incorporated documents, were written in Hebrew, and that the same translator rendered them into Greek. A careful study of the literary characteristics also shows the work of one author throughout. The letters, treaties, etc., are shown to be free reproductions and paraphrases of actual documents which are here given a literary shaping. Not one of them can be regarded as interpolated by a later hand. The book should mark a turning point in the criticism of First Maccabees.

As for Josephus, when his immediate purpose and his striving after brevity are taken into account, it will be seen that he could well dispense with chapters 14–16, which contain very little that would interest a Gentile historian. There was one item, however, that he could not bear to leave out, the incident of Numenius and the golden shield "of a thousand pounds weight" which the Jews presented to the Romans, and he accordingly (and characteristically) introduced it in his history at a convenient place. It is he who is at fault, and the substantial trustworthiness of the older historian is not to be questioned.

Literature. See §9; also H. W. Ettelson, *The Integrity of I Maccabees* (1925). E. R. Bevan, "Syria and the Jews," *Cambridge Ancient History*, VIII (1930), 495–533.

§18. Second Maccabees

This "Second" book is said by its author, in 2:23, to be the abridgment of a larger work consisting of "five books" composed by one Jason of Cyrene. Beyond this statement nothing is known concerning the latter. The Epitomist says in effect, in 2:25–28, that his own labors consisted solely in abridging and popularizing Jason's history.

Prefixed to the epitome, but formally connected with it (see 2:19), is a highly interesting introduction consisting of two letters purporting to have been sent by the Jews of Jerusalem and Judea to the Jews of Egypt. Since these letters are quite distinct from the main body of the book and are plainly not the work of its author (though translated into Greek and prefixed by him, as will appear), they will be treated separately.

Second Maccabees is a history of the Hasmonean uprising, differing widely from First Maccabees both in general character and in contents. The events with which it deals are all included in a period of little more than fifteen years, from a time shortly previous to the accession of Antiochus Epiphanes (175 B.C.) down to the year 160. It is thus in the main parallel to 1 Macc. 1–7. The contents are as follows: Author's preface (2:19–32). Story of Heliodorus, whose attempt to plunder the temple at Jerusalem was miraculously thwarted (chap. 3). Account of the intrigues by which the high priesthood changed hands, the misdeeds of Simon the overseer of the temple and the renegade high priests Jason and Menelaus (chap. 4). The calamities that came upon Jerusalem when Jason captured the city and butchered many of the inhabitants. Antiochus, returning from Egypt, makes a great slaughter in the city and plunders the temple (chap. 5). Judas Maccabeus and his brethren flee to the mountains (5:27). The persecution of the Jews, begun in 168. Story of the martyrdom of Eleazar, and of the seven youths with their mother (chaps. 6 and 7). The remainder of the book (chaps. 8–15) is taken up with the account of the wars waged by Judas. The correspondences with First Maccabees are sometimes close, but often of only a very general character. The book closes with the great victory gained by Judas and his army over the hated Syrian general Nicanor in the battle of Beth Horon, 160 B.C.

Students of the book are generally agreed that the sources at the disposal of Jason of Cyrene must have been mainly oral. The account that he gives is sometimes confused and even self-contradictory, though at the same time bearing marks of authenticity. Examples are given in the commentaries. The order of events is now and then plainly disturbed, as in the statements regarding the Syrian captain Timotheus, whose death is narrated in 10:37, while he appears again repeatedly in chapter 12. Yet the narrative in both of these chapters contains such vivid touches—especially in unimportant incidents—as suggest the recollection of eye-witnesses. See for example 10:37 and 12:35. It is evident that Jason's information was not often obtained from men who had themselves taken part in the Maccabean wars, but came to him through other hands. He wrote in one of the lands of the Dispersion, and had not the means of criticising and arranging the "dense mass" (2:24) of material at his disposal. See also under First Maccabees.

That which the Epitomist says of his own work, in 2:25–29 (cf. 6:12–16), was doubtless true also of Jason's history, that it kept in view the edification and entertainment of the Jewish people. The probability of a story was a matter of little importance if it was interesting and patriotic. Examples are numerous. In 13:15–23 the defeats suffered by Judas and his allies in the year 162 (1 Macc. 6:47–54) are made a series of brilliant victories for the Jews. Miracles are given a very prominent place in the narrative, and from the amount of space which they occupy it seems plain that this feature also belonged to Jason's work. With all its defects, however, this "Second" book is a valuable history, and there are points where its disjointed story may be preferred to the orderly scheme of the "First" book.

Religious teaching has a prominent part in the history, as has already been implied. Its most interesting feature is the repeated expression of faith in the resurrection of the dead; see especially 12:43–45, and compare 7:9, 11, 14, 36; 14:46. In no other of the few passages in pre-Christian Jewish literature in which this belief appears is it so clearly and emphatically expressed.

An important aim of the history, religious and political, was to bring about a more perfect unity of the Jews. There was need of strengthening among the Jews of the Dispersion the feeling of national pride and of enthusiasm for the stated observances, of the consciousness of close connection with the brethren in the holy land. The account of the celebration of the great victory, and of the institution of the Nicanor festival of the 13th of Adar, with which the whole history comes to an end, was the natural point for Jason to bring his book to a close. He had no need to go on and narrate the death of Judas. The prominence given to the account of the re-dedication of the temple and the annual observance of the day (10:8) served the same purpose; these were the two *Maccabean* feasts, by the observance of which the Jews of the Dispersion could share in the national glory of the great struggle and triumph.

The emphasis on this latter account, which in Second Maccabees closes the first half of the book, may be due especially to the Epitomist, whose marked interest in the feast is shown by his prefixing the two Letters to his abridgment (see below), and to his charge may perhaps be laid the transposition of the passage 10:1–8 from its true place in the history (see 1 Macc. 4:36 ff.) to its present significant position after the death of Antiochus.

Regarding the literary character of Second Maccabees, little need be said here. It is written in the inflated and tiresome Greek of the Ptolemaic period by a man of learning and skill. The most common faults of this school of writers, an overloaded and artificial style, and an ill-judged striving after rhetorical effect, are not absent. Details are exaggerated, scenes are painted at undue length (e.g., 3:15–22), the enemies of the Jews are mentioned with abusive epithets, and the writer's own reflections are given an unnecessary amount of space. A fair idea of the style can be gained by reading (in any language) the long-winded prologue, 2:19–32.

The Epitomist evidently wrote in Egypt, presumably at Alexandria. For a conjecture as to the date of his work we have only the help of the prefixed Letters. For determining the date of Jason's history there is the allusion in 15:36 to the "day of Mordecai" and the story of Esther. The matter is complicated by new facts which have come to light in regard to the book of Esther; see "The Older Book of Esther," *Harvard Theol. Rev., 37* (1944), 38–40, where Jason's work is dated conjecturally at about 130 B.C. The date of the second of the Letters prefixed to the epitome is 124 B.C., and on all accounts it now seems probable that Second Maccabees was written soon after this date.

A. *The Prefixed Letters*

These purport to be official letters sent from Jerusalem to the Jews of Egypt, calling to the celebration of the feast of the Dedication of the Temple on the 25th of the month Chislev. There is no good reason for questioning the genuineness of the two letters, and there are strong grounds for believing them authentic. They were written in Aramaic, the natural language for such communications, and (as is very evident) they were rendered into Greek by the Epitomist himself. The second letter follows the first without a pause, and is itself articulated to the following history in 2:19 by the Greek particle δέ.

In the standard commentaries and textbooks, as well as in some editions of the Greek text, the division between the letters is made in the wrong place. The date at the beginning of verse 10, "In the 188th year" (that is, in the year 124 B.C.), belongs to the following letter, not to the preceding. The date of the *first* letter is in verse 7, and the true reading in verses 7 and 8 is as follows: "In the reign of Demetrius, in the year 169,[69] we the Jews write to you [this letter]. In the distress and the affliction which came upon us in those years after Jason and those with him withdrew . . . and they shed innocent blood, we besought the Lord and were accepted," etc.[70] The letter is brief, and makes the impression of a routine announcement.

The *second* letter, 1:10–2:18, is much longer and a document of great interest. It is sent by the men of Jerusalem and Judea and the senate of the Jews (not, "the senate *and Judas*"!)[71] to Aristobulus and the Jewish leaders in Egypt. It undertakes to show the important place in the history of Israel occupied by the Feast of the Dedication, and the stature of Judas Maccabaeus as a national hero. Judas is the successor of Moses, Solomon, and Nehemiah in the matter of the fire on Yahweh's altar; like Jeremiah and Nehemiah he collected and preserved sacred things which were in danger of perishing.

The principal matters treated in the letter are the following: 1. Death of Antiochus (Sidetes) in Persia, where he was seeking to rob a temple of Nanai (2:11–17). 2. How Nehemiah built a temple and an altar in Babylonia, and re-kindled the sacred fire (1:18b–36). 3. How Jeremiah concealed the tabernacle, the ark, and the altar of incense in a cave in the mountain (2:4–8). 4. Relation of Solomon and Moses to the Feast of Dedication ((2:8b–12). 5. How Nehemiah collected a sacred library (namely, Chronicles, Ezra, and his own book!), and how Judas made a similar collection (2:13–15).

Because of the fact that each of the two dates, 143 and 124 B.C., marks a time of especial rejoicing in Palestine and Egypt, a triumph of *all* the Jews, and possibly a notable celebration in the latter country, it has been conjectured that the two letters were preserved and kept together by some one, and that thus they came into the hands of the Epitomist. To the latter they seemed so important that he made them an integral part of his work.[72]

Literature. See §9; also Torrey, "The Letters Prefixed to Second Maccabees," *Jour. Am. Or. Soc., 60* (1940), 119–150 (with an attempted restoration of the Aramaic text of both letters).

69. That is, the year 143 B.C.

70. "Translation-Greek" has been fatally misleading in this passage!

71. The letter must have been copied (in Aramaic) very often, from the time of its arrival in Egypt. The copy which came into the hands of our Epitomist had been somewhat carelessly transcribed, and contains a number of errors.

72. The customary place for the date of a letter, at the time when these were written, is at the end, not at the beginning. The possibility may be considered that the Epitomist transferred the date of the second letter, for it would have rendered impossible the transition at 2:19 which he had planned.

§19. Third Maccabees

THE book is an edifying short story having for its subject the triumph of the Jews over their enemies through divine intervention. It was classed in church lists as "Maccabean" merely because it is a narrative of persecution by a foreign king. It professes to record events which occurred during the reign of Ptolemy IV Philopator (222–204 B.C.), out of whose hands the Jews of Egypt are delivered by a series of marvelous occurrences. The narrative runs as follows.

After Ptolemy's victory over Antiochus the Great at Raphia (217 B.C.), he visits Jerusalem and tries to enter the temple, in spite of the frantic opposition of priests and people. Just as he is on the point of executing his evil purpose he is stricken from heaven and falls to the ground (1:1–2:24). Returning to Alexandria, bent on revenge, he assembles the Jews of Egypt and shuts them up in the great hippodrome, where they are all to be butchered. It is however first necessary to record their names. This proves to be an endless task, because of their immense number; before it can be finished the supply of writing materials in Egypt is exhausted, and the Jews are saved for the time being (2:25–4:21).

The king then devises a new plan. Five hundred elephants, made furious with wine, are to be let loose upon the Jews in the hippodrome. The execution of the order, however, is hindered in various ways. On the first day the king oversleeps. On the second day, being caused by God to forget all that had happened, he calls the Jews his best friends, and reproves those who would remind him of his decree. Finally, on the third day, as the sentence is about to be executed, two angels appear, terrifying the king and his officers and causing the elephants to turn upon the men of the royal army and trample them to death (5:1–6:21).

The scale is now completely turned in favor of the Jews. They are forthwith set free; the king provides for them a great banquet lasting seven days; and an official proclamation in their favor is sent forth to all the generals and other high officers of Egypt (the text of this royal letter is given in 7:1–9). With the king's permission the Jews now kill more than three hundred renegades of their nation, and then return to their homes with great joy. A monument is erected in memory of their deliverance, and the days on which it was effected are set apart to be celebrated henceforth (6:22–7:23).

It is plain from the foregoing synopsis that the book contains little more than a series of incredible fables. It is to be noticed that Jo-

sephus (*Contra Apionem*, ii, 5) has the same story, but in a later form
and in another historical setting. Here, the royal enemy is Ptolemy
VII Physcon (146–117 B.C.). The king, it is said, assembled and
bound all the Jews of Alexandria, and exposed them to be trampled to
death by his elephants, which he had made drunk. But the furious
beasts turned upon his own men and killed many of them. The king
also saw "a fearful apparition" (compare the incident of the angels
in Third Maccabees) which made him cease from his purpose. It is
added, that the Jews of Alexandria have been accustomed to celebrate
the day of their deliverance.

Josephus was evidently unacquainted with Third Maccabees, and
the conclusion would seem to be that a memory-version of the tale
came into his hands. It does not fit well into his history. There is no
valid reason for supposing that any such feast was ever celebrated
by the Jews of Alexandria; this set feature is imitated from Second
Maccabees, Esther, Judith, and perhaps still other narratives. The
only historical information that can be gained from the book is that
which can be inferred regarding the condition of the Jews of Egypt
at the time when it was written. It is plain that they felt themselves
to be in hostile surroundings, that they were harassed, if not openly
persecuted, and that the number of those who deserted to the Gentiles
was not small.

It is evident that the book as we have it is not complete, the beginning is missing. This appears not only from the opening words, ὁ δὲ
Φιλοπάτωρ, but also from a number of distinct allusions to a preceding
portion of narrative which our book no longer contains. The most
striking examples are the following: 1:1, "from those who returned";
1:2, "the (above mentioned) plot"; 2:25, "the boon companions already mentioned."

Now it is clear that the story is concerned mainly with the triumph
of the Jews over their persecutors, and the probability is strong that
the missing portion was of the same general character as 1:1–7, that
is, it formed with it the introduction to the story. It must have included some mention of the following items: 1. character of Ptolemy
and his companions; 2. antecedents of the war with Antiochus III;
3. condition of the Jews in Egypt (perhaps); 4. the plot against
Ptolemy's life. All of this might have been contained in a single short
chapter, and it is probable that this much and no more has been acci-
dentally lost. At the beginning of the book, we may conjecture, a
single leaf of a codex fell out.

The original language of Third Maccabees was Greek, beyond
question. Its author had at his command an unusually large vocabulary (see the Introduction in Grimm's *Commentary*) and considerable

resources of rhetoric; but the faults of this Alexandrian school of writers, mentioned above in the description of Second Maccabees, are here seen at their worst. The style is bombastic and inflated to the last degree, everything is flourished and exaggerated. This is not Greek that can be read with pleasure.

The author of the book was a Jew of Alexandria, beyond much doubt. The date of his work cannot be conjectured very definitely. It gives evidence of acquaintance with Second Maccabees (see the commentaries), and in 6:6 is cited the book of Daniel in its later form, with the apocryphal additions. Some time near the end of the last century B.C. would perhaps be the most likely date.

Literature. See §9.

§20. Tobit

It has often been said that the book of Tobit has in its plot the framework of a complete novel. As a "short story" it has been more popular than any other of the Jewish compositions of this class. In its Greek translation, in the lands of the Dispersion but first of all and prevailingly in Egypt, it circulated widely in slightly differing editions, sometimes reproduced from memory, as was the case with all the popular narratives.

The Christians, adopting the Greek scriptures of the Old Testament and at first paying little attention to the question of canonical authority, made eager use of the Jewish religious narratives, both for private edification and for church reading. In their Bible, which soon began to take shape (in codex form; see the General Introduction) the books of Tobit and Judith were given a place between Nehemiah and Esther. This was true also, from the first, in the Latin Bible.

The usual form of the name, "Tobit" ending in -*t* (or sometimes -*th*), is Greek. The Hebrew name was Tōbī, and the Greek added the final consonant in order to make it indeclinable, as in the case of numerous other foreign words which inconveniently ended in a vowel. Tobit's son is named Tobias (Hebrew Tōbīyāh), and the two names must be kept distinct; they are sometimes confused in the Greek manuscripts and regularly in the Latin Vulgate, where each is given as Tobias.

The events of the narrative take place in the eastern part of the Assyrian empire, between Nineveh on the Tigris and the Median city Rages (Rhagae), south of the Caspian Sea. The time of the principal action is the reign of Esarhaddon (680–668 B.C.). Tobit, a native of

Kadesh-Naphtali, was carried in his youth to Assyria in the principal deportation of the people of the Northern Kingdom in 722 by Sargon (who by the narrator is consistently called Shalmaneser, see 1:2, 13, 15 f.). His fellow tribesmen of Naphtali had been idolaters—like the rest of northern Israel; but he, under the instruction of his grandmother Deborah, had kept the Mosaic laws and ordinances. Brought to Nineveh, he eventually gained the favorable notice of the king, who made him his purveyor. It was here, some time after the deportation,[73] that he took a wife, Anna, of his own family, and she bore him Tobias. In the days of his prosperity he went to Media, and left there ten talents of silver (say, $20,000) in trust with his cousin Gabael.

Sennacherib, Sargon's son and successor (cf. 1:15), slew many Hebrews in his rage and would leave them unburied. Tobit, daring to bury some of them secretly, is informed against and obliged to flee for his life, while all his property is confiscated.[74] The reign of Esarhaddon brought a change for the better. Tobit's own nephew, Ahikar (famous in eastern literature; see below), was the king's trusted counselor and administrator; a word from him to the king brought the fugitive back to Nineveh, and he was restored to his wife and son.

Here the action of the story begins. Tobit again has occasion to bury one of his murdered countrymen, and in the resulting circumstances he becomes blind, by a strange accident. Four years elapse, his condition proves hopeless, and in addition he is reduced to poverty; for Ahikar, who had supported him, has been obliged to leave Nineveh and to reside temporarily in Elymais. Anna now supports the family by taking in work of dressmaking for well-to-do women of the city. After a lively scene in which Tobit, disheartened and distrustful, accuses his wife of stealing, he retires to pray to God for release from his misery. Confessing his unworthiness, he asks to have his life taken from him.

The scene now shifts for a moment to the city Ecbatana in Media, where the daughter of a good Hebrew family is in sore distress. Sought in marriage by the young men of her people, she has yet gained no husband, for the demon Asmodaeus has killed each of her suitors, in

73. The ‫א‬ text of 1:9 f. has a false division of the verses.

74. To account for the calamities that must come upon the hero of the story, it was necessary for its author to think of some righteous act which would antagonize and anger the king. An effective solution was found in Tobit's devotion to the duty of burying the dead of his people, who in this foreign land might be slain and cast out without burial. He had buried such in the time of Sargon (1:17); because of Sennacherib's wrath at the Hebrews the pious custom nearly cost him his life; and under Esarhaddon, from whom he had nothing to fear, his attention to the same duty was the indirect cause of his losing his eyesight. This is skillful use of a purely Hebrew motive suggested by the requirement of the story. Some features of this famous narrative have been borrowed in later folk-tales.

the wedding night, until seven have been thus disposed of. The maid-servants of the house not only taunt her with childlessness, but also accuse her of having murdered her husbands. In the extremity of her despair, she goes up to her chamber, opens the window toward Jerusalem, and prays to be taken from the earth, unless some help is reserved for her. While she was uttering her petition in Ecbatana, Tobit's was being uttered in Nineveh; at the moment when he ceased and returned to his family, Sarah the daughter of Raguel came down from her chamber. "And the prayer of both was heard before the great glory, and Raphael was sent to heal them both."

The action is now resumed at Nineveh. Tobit, remembering the money deposited at Rages, suddenly realizes that his son Tobias is old enough to go and get it. The search for a guide and companion for the long and dangerous journey results in hiring the angel Raphael, who assumes the name and form of a man of Naphtali, the son of one of Tobit's old acquaintances. After the father had given his son some wise counsel, and the things needful for the journey had been prepared, the two set out on their way, "and the young man's dog went with them." This last clause is heard with a certain shock, for it is opposed to the uniform Hebrew tradition, which excludes the dog from good society; but the narrator had his wise purpose in making the animal one of the party.

At the first halting place for the night, on the bank of the Tigris, Tobias has the good fortune to snatch a large fish from the river. This yields them good food, and much more. The guide, "Azariah," gives the youth mysterious directions: Take the heart, liver, and gall of the fish; the heart and liver to drive away a devil or evil spirit, and the gall to remove white films from the eyes of a blind man.

The further progress of the story is now evident. When the travelers come to Ecbatana, Sarah is found to be Tobias' cousin, the one among all women whom it was fittest for him to marry. Objections and fears are overcome, and the wedding is duly celebrated. Asmodaeus appears at the customary time, but the smoke of the heart and liver, burned by Tobias on a censer, drives him away to the most distant part of the earth, upper Egypt. The grave dug by Raguel and his servants, to receive the body of Tobias, is found to be unnecessary. Azariah, provided with the necessary documents, is sent on to Rages, and before the fourteen days of the wedding festivities are over he returns with the ten talents, bringing also Gabael to take part in the celebration.

In the house at Nineveh there is mourning, for many days have gone by since the time appointed for the return of Tobias. The despairing mother watches the road, and one day sees Tobias' dog approaching. Tobit hears her cries of joy and stumbles out through the door in time to meet his son and Azariah; for they were alone. When the returning travelers had reached the city which lies across the river from Nineveh (see below), Tobias and his guide, by the advice of the latter, had gone forward in advance of the others, while the dog, now in sight of his home, had scampered on before them.[75] Tobias, with the gall of the fish in his hand, smears his father's eyes and restores his sight. Sarah and her retinue, now at the gate of Nineveh, are joyfully welcomed; there is another wedding feast, at which Ahikar and his nephew Nadan are present. Thereafter Azariah makes himself known to the family as the angel Raphael. The book closes with Tobit's prayer of thanksgiving (originally in metric form) occupying the entire thirteenth chapter, and with his last words of counsel to his children.

The story from beginning to end is distinctly in the atmosphere of Babylonia and Persia; no other document in Bible or apocrypha makes a like impression. It is true that a writer in Palestine or Egypt or elsewhere might be acquainted with every detail contained in the narrative, but the presumption that the author of the book was a Babylonian Jew is nevertheless clear, even if it cannot be proved.

The date has generally been regarded, with good reason, as pre-Maccabean. The work of the Chronicler in the book of Ezra (middle of the 3d century B.C.) is plainly referred to in 14:5.[76] A time two or three decades subsequent to this would seem to be the most likely date for the composition of the book of Tobit.

The history of Ahikar, the counselor of Sennacherib and Esarhaddon, and especially the wise maxims of the sage,[77] are drawn upon and imitated by the author of the tale of Tobit. The casual manner of the allusion to Nadan's treachery, and to the punishment which finally overtook him, in 14:10, shows that the author of the tale wrote where the story of the wise Ahikar was familiar to everyone.[78] For the words of wisdom put into Tobit's mouth, see especially chapter 4. The Ahikar literature from which our author quoted must have been very popular in the Mesopotamian lands from the time (probably the sixth century) when it was composed. Its original language was presumably

75. Thus in Fritzsche's "third" Greek text (here the oldest form extant) and in the Syriac version. See 11:13 in Fritzsche's edition, p. 146, below. This charming touch in the narrative has disappeared from the other known texts.

76. This is the earliest allusion in any Hebrew or Jewish document, outside the Chronicler's own work, to a return from the Babylonian exile.

77. See the translation of the extensive fragments found at Elephantine, in Cowley's *Aramaic Papyri of the Fifth Century B.C.*, pp. 220–226.

78. The ridiculously impossible "Manasses"(!) in this verse is simply a familiar Aramaic participle with its suffixed pronoun, *mᵉnassēh*, "His benefactor," the one who had given him his favored position, cf. Esther 3:1, 5:11!

Aramaic, there is no good reason for any other supposition. This was the language of the people, and their literary medium, even under the later Assyrian kings. The attempts to show the original to have been Persian, or Hebrew, or Babylonian cuneiform, are all equally unconvincing.

An interesting question, of some importance, relates to the location of the city in which the author of the tale of Tobit lays its principal scenes. Had he in mind the real Nineveh, on the upper Tigris? The present writer, in an article published in the *Jour. Bib. Lit., 41* (1922), 237–245, argued that the city supposed to have been Nineveh was really Seleucia. There are indeed very strong reasons for this conclusion. It is common knowledge that the site of Nineveh was early forgotten and remained unknown; thus even in the time of Xenophon, 400 B.C. The Jewish authorities of the Babylonian Talmud located the five typical Assyrian cities of Genesis 10:11, Asshur, Nineveh, Rehoboth-Ir, Calah, and Resen, *all in Babylonia,* identifying them with Seleucia, "Nineveh" (where?) Perath-Mesene, Borsippa, and Ctesiphon. There was no idea of a kingdom farther up the Tigris. It now seems to be the case (as would be expected) that the Babylonian Jews of the 3d century B.C. held the same view regarding the location of Assyria.

When Tobias and his party returned from the east, they had to cross the Tigris river in order to reach their home. This is made clear in the best texts, the longer Greek, the Syriac, and the Old Latin, in 11:1. But the true Nineveh was on the east side of the river! Also, *directly opposite* their "Nineveh," across the Tigris, lay another city through which they must pass, its corrupted name variously given in the different sources. Here Tobias with his guide goes on ahead of the others, to prepare his parents for the arrival of the caravan; and it is obvious that he could not have left his wife behind at any greater distance from home than this. There was only one such pair of cities on the river, namely Seleucia and Ctesiphon. When we first hear of the latter city, in 221 B.C., its importance is chiefly that of a halting station for the caravans coming from the north or the east to bring their wares to Seleucia across the river; see Pauly-Wissowa, *Real-Encyclopädie*, Supplement, *s.v.* "Ktesiphon," Col. 1110. Once more: When Tobias and the angel set out on their journey, their first stopping place for the night is on the Tigris. If they had started from the real Nineveh, they could not have come to the Tigris at all. Starting from Seleucia, the caravan road goes due north from Ctesiphon, and our travelers would touch the Tigris at just the right time and place. The conclusion seems certain, Tobit's "Nineveh" was Seleucia.

The Greek of Tobit is very obviously the result of translation. The

original language is shown by many plain indications to have been
Aramaic. A case in point is the "Manasses" of 14:10, mentioned above.
The Aramaic word gives exactly the form of the proper name; the
mistake would not have been possible in Hebrew. There is no space
here for other examples.

The best available Greek text of the book is that of the Sinaitic
manuscript (א), though it is corrupt and defective. It is printed in
Swete's LXX in smaller type on the lower half of the page. An English translation (with little attempt at criticism) is given by D. C.
Simpson in Charles's *Apocrypha and Pseudepigrapha*. The text ordinarily printed and translated, as in our English Apocrypha, is that
of the Vatican manuscript (Codex B). It is systematically abridged
throughout, as can easily be shown, and lacks some important features
of the narrative. Many of its readings, however, are superior to those
of the Sinaitic manuscript. A third form of the Greek, old and important but likewise yielding an abridged text, is preserved only in the
portion 6:10–13:18.[79] From these three a good eclectic text (greatly
needed) based on א could be made. All forms of the Greek originated
in a single translation, and there is much evidence of mutual con-
tamination.

An interesting literary feature of the book is the use of the first person in the first three chapters (thus in all forms of the text), the
author identifying himself in imagination with his hero, at first, and
thus adding appreciably to the verisimilitude of the narration. This
is done with similar effect in the Old Testament, in Ezra, chapters 8
and 9; while in Neh. 10:31–40 (Engl. version, 30–39), also belonging
to the Ezra narrative, is employed the first person plural, suggested
by the closing words of Ezra's prayer in chapter 9.

At the end of the book there is a passage, 14:15, generally overlooked or misunderstood, which is historically important. Tobias, we
are told, died at Ecbatana of Media, being a hundred and twenty-
seven years old. "And before he died he heard of the destruction of
Nineveh, which Nebuchadnezzar *and Ahasuerus* took captive." This is
the reading of the standard version. In the longer version the capture
of the city is ascribed to "Ahikar(!) the king of Media." The original
reading of this version also was probably Ahasuerus, as Simpson, in
Charles's *Apocrypha*, decides. Some scribe thought to improve upon it.

Nineveh was destroyed by Nabopolassar *and Cyaxares;* and there
are several items of clear evidence showing that the Jewish writers of

79. This text formed the basis of the second half (i.e., from 7:11b onward) of the
Syriac version. A trace of the lost earlier portion of this Greek is perhaps to be found
in the interesting Old Latin manuscript C, which from 1:1 to 6:12 is derived from a
Greek text much like the Sinaitic, but thereafter merely adopts the Vulgate.

the last few centuries B.C. confused the name Ahasuerus (Xerxes) with the Median name. "Darius the Mede"—that is, Darius Hystaspis, made to precede Cyrus—was believed to be the son of the great Cyaxares ("Ahasuerus," Dan. 9:1!); and *his* son Xerxes, "of the seed of the Medes," was naturally supposed to bear the name of his grandfather. The author of the book of Tobit gave in this passage the current Jewish doctrine.

Literature. See §9; also the article on the site of "Nineveh," mentioned above.

§21. Judith

This is a fine example of a Jewish popular tale. The proud city "Bethulia" is besieged by the army of Nebuchadnezzar. The water supply is cut off by the besiegers, and the rulers of the city are about to surrender. "Yet five days," is the decree; then, if no help comes, the city shall be given over to the enemy. Judith,[80] a wealthy and beautiful widow of noble descent, famed in the city for her piety, rebukes the rulers for their lack of faith, and asks for permission to carry out her plan, the nature of which she cannot divulge.

The commander of the hostile army, Holofernes, is enjoying himself while preparing for the kill. He has had fair warning from an unprejudiced witness in his own army, Achior the Ammonite, that the city cannot be taken if its people keep the law of their god. Holofernes responds by having Achior bound hand and foot and deposited at the foot of the hill on which Bethulia stands; he may perish along with the doomed Hebrews. The army now moves up under the city; Holofernes pitches his tent in the valley.

Judith prepared for action, first, by fasting and prayer; then, by discarding sackcloth and the garments of widowhood and bringing forth her finest apparel; "she decked herself bravely, to beguile the eyes of all men that should see her." With her maid, who carried food and drink sufficient for several days, she set off down the hill and entered the camp of the enemy. Both the guard and Holofernes, to whom she is conducted, are so overcome by her beauty that they do whatever she tells them to do. She professes to have information which will enable the general to take the city, without the loss of even one of his men, at the time, now close at hand, when she gives the word.

80. The name ("Jewess") suggests, and doubtless was intended to suggest, her representative character. See below, in regard to 16:1.

On the evening of the fourth day Judith appeared to yield herself
to Holofernes, and joined him at a private banquet, eating and drink-
ing however only what her maid provided. He, in his exultation, drank
so heavily that he became an easy prey. At midnight, Judith and her
maid went out through the camp to the brook below the city, as they
had done on each preceding night. The sentries, under instructions, let
them pass. This time, however, the bag which they were wont to carry
contained the head of Holofernes, and instead of returning from the
brook to the camp they went up the hill to the city. At the voice of
Judith the gates are opened; a bonfire is soon blazing; men with
torches rush from all directions; Achior the Ammonite identifies the
head of the tyrant. All the city is in an uproar, and a great shout of
triumph goes up.

At dawn, the armed men of Bethulia pour out upon the brow of the
hill, in ordered ranks, as though preparing to attack. The besiegers
are at first surprised, then uneasy, as they wait impatiently for some
word of command. When at length the news is heard in all the camp,
"Holofernes lieth upon the ground, and his head is not on him," there
is panic in the army and all flee in disorder in every direction. The
men of Bethulia pursue, and take great spoil. The high priest and the
elders of Jerusalem come to Bethulia, to have sight of Judith and to
give her their blessing. At the celebration there, a month later, a psalm
of thanksgiving is sung; Judith, impersonating all Israel,[81] leading
the chant, and the women of Bethulia responding in chorus. With the
text of the psalm (16 vss.), and a few words concerning the last days
of the heroine, the book ends.

These events are imagined to have taken place after the return of
the Jews from the captivity, and after the rebuilding of the temple
(4:3; 5:19). This is indefinite enough, and the narrator warns against
any desire to make it more definite. He takes pains to tell his hearers
plainly that they are listening to fiction, not to an account of actual
happenings. Those were the days when Nebuchadnezzar "reigned over
the Assyrians in Nineveh," and when Arphaxad "reigned over the
Medes in Ecbatana" (1:1). Here he gives his auditors a solemn wink.
It is just as though a modern story-teller should say: It happened at
the time when Napoleon Bonaparte was king of England, and Otto
von Bismarck was on the throne in Mexico. The Jewish novelist shows
his humor, as well as his care for the right appreciation of his work.[82]

81. The Greek text at this point does not seem to have been understood correctly by
any translator or commentator.

82. The humor and its purpose are quite lost on our modern commentators, who, without exception, believe the author of the narrative to be aiming to give it a real historical setting, and are astonished at his ignorance.

He knew that the readers and hearers of his own day, the young and the old alike, would see his meaning.

The story of Judith is edifying fiction, a favorite class of literature in pre-Christian Palestine. It is evidently designed to entertain as well as to instruct, and it is well fitted to accomplish both purposes. The author's chief interest, indeed, seems to have been in the story itself, rather than in any teaching to be gained from it. It is carefully constructed, exciting in its details, and conceived with the vivid imagination characteristic of the best Hebrew narrators. The principal characters are all fictitious, excepting "Joakim the high priest," who is evidently the one named in Neh. 12:10. The name Holofernes (Orophernes) was familiar in Palestine since the middle of the 4th century B.C., when a Persian general of that name led an army through Phoenicia into Egypt.

The main characteristics of the heroine of this tale were a matter of course. The narrator emphasizes the piety of Judith, and her strict observance of the laws and ordinances; he also portrays her as brave and resourceful, and as possessed of much practical wisdom. It is another quality, however, that is especially prominent in his narrative. He is very aware of the one thing that gives the story its measure of plausibility, Judith's extraordinary beauty, with her consciousness of its power; it was this weapon that saved the city.

As Judith goes forth on her desperate errand, and passes by the three chief men of Bethulia, they "wonder at her beauty very exceedingly." The men at the city gate could not turn their eyes from her; they "looked after her, until she was gone down the mountain, until she had passed the valley, and they could see her no more." The guards at the Assyrian camp had never seen such beauty; they chose a hundred men to escort her to the general's tent, and a crowd followed and "compassed her about and marvelled at her beauty." The Hebrews, they said, must be exterminated; if they have such women as this, "they will be able to deceive the whole earth." The effect on Holofernes is succinctly described in the psalm in the sixteenth chapter. Verse 7:

> It was not the sons of the Titans that smote him,
> Nor did towering giants attack him,
> But Judith the daughter of Merari
> paralyzed him with the beauty of her face.

And again, verse 9:

> Her loveliness took his soul captive—
> And the sword went through his neck.

In one important property of the Judith story, the geography and topography of the principal scenes, its author is dealing with reality, not with fiction. "Bethulia" is a pseudonym for Shechem, as was shown and recognized many years ago. The narrator was personally familiar with the city and with its surroundings, both the near and the more remote. It may well be that the site itself suggested to him the outline of the story. This was an old and famed Israelite city; it stood squarely in the pass by which a hostile army would approach Judea; the easy possibility of cutting off its water supply was obvious; also, the abundant springs below the city on the west side would suffice for an army encamped there. How much exaggeration there may have been in the account of the city's fortification (an ascent wide enough "for two men only," 4:7) it is fruitless now to conjecture.

The reason for the pseudonym is obvious. Because of the bitterly hostile feeling of the Jews toward the Samaritans, the name "Shechem" could not be repeatedly used in a popular tale of this character as that of the city whose people wrought deliverance for Jerusalem and for the sanctuary of the Jews. The author is nevertheless at pains to make the identity of the city plain even to those to whom the topographical details could give no clue. Judith is of the tribe of Simeon, which in the Hebrew tradition took possession of the city when "the Shechemites" were exterminated (5:16). Ozias, the chief ruler of Bethulia, is also of this tribe. Judith makes express mention, in 9:2 ff., of the narrative in Genesis 34, the account of the slaughter at Shechem. The writer's purpose to play on the city's history is also furthered—and his humor is again shown—by his making the name of Judith's deceased husband Manasseh(!), the most notorious and detested of the Samaritan names connected with Shechem.

The original form and meaning of the pseudonym are alike uncertain. Our "Bethulia" is a mere Latin adaptation; the best attested reading of the name is Betylua (Βαιτυλουα). The first element in this is *beth*, "house," but the remainder offers a riddle which hitherto has had no satisfactory solution. Beth Eloah, "House of God," has occasionally been proposed, but to this there are evident objections. The archaic form of the divine name is unlikely to have been used. The familiar word could hardly have been transliterated in this way! It is not likely that the name "House of God" would have been chosen for Shechem by a Jewish narrator, even in such a tale. On the other hand, an ill-omened epithet, however natural (see below), would have been unsuitable. Since all our Greek texts come from a single translation, and since the confusion of the letters *yod* and *waw* is very common, the conjecture seems plausible that *Beth*ᵉ*liya*, meaning "lofty abode," [83]

---

83. Literally, "house of ascent"; this is the late Hebrew (and Aramaic) nomen actionis *ᵉliyā;* see Levy, *Neuhebr. u. chald. Wörterbuch,* III, 652, where the first and typical meaning is given as "ascent" (Hinaufsteigen).

was miswritten as *Beth⁽ᵉ⁾luwa,* which would give exactly the standard Greek transliteration. Such a descriptive name would be most natural.

"Bethulia" (Betheliya) is not the only pseudonym in the story. There was another highly important city, near Shechem and likewise hated by the Jews, which was certain to be mentioned in this narrative which names so many of the principal towns of this neighborhood. When it is said in 4:6 that Joakim the high priest wrote from Jerusalem "to them that dwelt in Bethulia and Betomasthem," [84] charging them to defend the pass against the armies of Holofernes, the two cities intended are certainly Shechem and *Samaria.* The nickname of the latter city was either "Place of Enmity," *Beth mastēmā,* [85] or perhaps better, as agreeing with the Greek, *Beth Masṭēm,* "Home of the Devil," with use of the strange and interesting name for Satan which occurs so often, sometimes as "Prince Mastēmā," [86] in the book of Jubilees, chapters 10, 17, 18, 19, 48, and 49. The undisguised pseudonym of Samaria was still another index pointing to Shechem as the home of Judith. The wish to execrate the latter city also must have been strong; the Greek text rendered by the Syriac version gave its name everywhere as "Home of the Phallus."

The original language of the book was Hebrew, written by a man of learning and literary taste. The Greek translation, an unusually able rendering, must have been made at an early date. Our best text is generally correct (except for the proper names), but can be improved at numerous points.

The frequent and conspicuous mention of Dothan (3:9, 4:6, 7:3, 18, and 8:3) makes the conjecture plausible that this city was the home of the author of the story. Any one of its residents would often have looked across "the great ridge ('saw') of Judea" (3:9), and have been familiar with the topography of Shechem and the road leading to Jerusalem. In 4:6, 7:18, and 8:3 the mention of Dothan seems quite gratuitous.

As to the date of the book, the post-Maccabean time is indicated by 3:8 and 6:2, where the allusion to Antiochus Epiphanes, and to his efforts to establish a state religion with himself as the deity, seems plain. It may also fairly be urged that such virtual glorification of Shechem as is inherent in the story of Judith would more easily be

---

84. The Greek manuscripts vary considerably in their writing of the name; the form here chosen seems most likely to have been the one used by the Greek translator.

85. First proposed by Professor A. Condamin, "Un Pseudonyme de Samarie dans le Livre de Judith," *Recherches de Science Religieuse* (Nov.-Déc., 1910), pp. 570 f.

86. The final -ā is the Aramaic determinative ending. "Prince *of the* Mastēmā," the reading given in some of the Ethiopic manuscripts and adopted by Charles, is wrong, since the original language of Jubilees was Aramaic, and the abstract noun could not have this form.

conceived by a narrator, and accepted by his audience, *after* John Hyrcanus had taken and humbled the city and destroyed the temple on Mount Gerizim than in the previous years when city and temple were a constant source of exasperation to the Jews.

~~Indeed,~~ it is hard to believe that such a story as this could have been written and published at any time when the Samaritans were prosperous and aggressive. Now we know of one time when they were utterly crushed, so that the Jews had no occasion to think of them as troublesome rivals. John Hyrcanus not only destroyed their temple on Mount Gerizim (about 120 B.C.) but also added greatly to his task of humbling them by razing Samaria to the ground. This was one of the last military deeds of his life (about the year 109), and the city was so thoroughly destroyed (see Josephus, *Antt.*, 13, x, 3!) that no attempt to restore it was made for nearly half a century. Some part of this period, while it was possible in Jewish Palestine to joke about the Samaritans and their cities—say, the first half of the last century B.C.—seems by far the most probable time for the composition of this lively tale. If the pseudonym of Samaria contains the name "Mastēm," as was conjectured above, this adds its support, for from the existing evidence it does not seem likely that this substitute for "Satan" was used as early as the 2d century B.C. ~~See the remarks on the name in the section on the book of Jubilees.~~

Literature. See §9; also two articles by the present writer: "The Site of Bethulia," *Jour. Am. Or. Soc., 20* (1899), 160–172 (the first recognition of Schechem as the city intended); "The Surroundings of 'Bethulia,'" *Florilegium Melchior de Vogüé* (Paris, 1909), pp. 599–605 (making doubly certain what was already assured).

§22. THE WISDOM OF SIRACH

THIS noble monument of the Hebrew wisdom literature stands at the head of all the "outside books." Its traditional Latin name, *Ecclesiasticus* (abbreviated Ecclus.), designates it as *the* "church book" *par excellence* in the extra-canonical literature, showing how highly it was esteemed in Christian circles from the earliest times. By the Jews also it was held in high honor. Though never regarded by them as canonical, it nevertheless was given a place of its own, and in the rabbinical writings is occasionally cited in the manner reserved for the sacred books.[87] By the Syriac-speaking Jews it was given an early translation

87. See Cowley and Neubauer, *The Original Hebrew of a Portion of Ecclesiasticus,* pp. XIX f.

based primarily on the Hebrew text, and it was included in the list of O. T. books even by the Nestorian Christians, who shunned the apocrypha; see the General Introduction, §6.

This is the only book of the extra-canonical literature whose author's name is known. In 50:27 we are given both name and residence; and eventually, as will be seen, the author tells us more about himself. He is Jesus the son of Sirach (Σειραχ), of Jerusalem.[88] We are fortunate also in knowing the time at which he lived, and the circumstances under which his book, composed in Hebrew, was translated into Greek.

The Greek text of the work is preceded by a Prologue, whose author introduces himself as the grandson of Jesus, and tells how, when he came to Egypt "in the 38th year of Euergetes the king," he found a copy of his grandfather's book and was moved to translate it for the instruction of the Greek-speaking Jews. Allusions in the body of the work make it certain that the king was Euergetes II (Ptolemy Physkon), whose 38th year was 132 B.C. It is therefore customary to say that Jesus bar Sīrā wrote his proverbs at about the year 180 B.C.

The proverbs are an admirable collection covering a wide range, written by a man of literary taste who had the gift of clear and forcible expression. We are given a remarkably comprehensive view of the wisdom of a learned and orthodox Jew of Palestine in the time just preceding the Maccabees. He is not concerned to recommend the religion of Israel, for he can take it for granted. Foremost among the things which all must recognize (42:1 ff.) is "the law of the Most High and his covenant," "the law of life and knowledge" (45:5). In chapters 1 and 2 he sums up all wisdom as the fear of the Lord; so also elsewhere, as in the fine poem 24:1–22, where Wisdom is personified in the customary manner. However, in the greater part of the space occupied by his proverbs it is to "worldly wisdom" that he pays attention. He is a theologian of rank, and a teacher of religious truth, but nonetheless a man of the world, proud of his practical philosophy. Put your trust in the Lord (32:24; 33:1), but trust also the wisdom that comes of experience.

His advice to the sick man, 38:1–15, may serve for partial illustration. My son, when you are ill pray to the Lord, and he will heal you. Cleanse your heart from sin, offer your sacrifice, and then put yourself in the hands of a physician, for God created him (this is said twice), let him not go from you. A wise man will not refuse to take medicines.

88. The original form of the (Semitic) name is Sīrā, the Greek consonant being added in order to make the word indeclinable, as in other similar cases; cf. especially *Akeldama(ch)* in the Greek of Acts 1:19.

The authority of years and experience is evident enough in all parts of the book, but we also have a bit of definite information given by the writer himself. He tells us in 34:11 f. that he has traveled abroad (see also 39:4 and 51:13) and has seen and learned many things, more than his words can show (vs. 11b). Once and again his life has been in danger. The passage 34:9–12 does not stand alone, but has interesting parallels. In chapter 38, in the contrast drawn between the man of learning (vs. 24) who wields influence in his city, and the ploughman in the country who can talk only of his bullocks (vs. 25), all commentators have seen that Bar Sira is thinking with satisfaction of his own favored status. Not that he could despise any laborer: the craftsman, the smith, the engraver, the potter, each absorbed, like the ploughman, in perfecting his own work (vss. 26–30), may not indeed sit high in the council of the people nor shine as teachers, "but they maintain the fabric of the world" (vs. 34).

It is equally evident in 39:1–11 that the writer has himself in mind, see also verses 12 and 32 f.; and another striking example is the epilogue 24:30–34 appended to the poem in praise of Wisdom. With these passages for guidance, it is clear that the entire closing section of the book, 50:27–51:30, refers definitely to the author himself, not to any wise man imagined by him. The only item of biography gained from it is an interesting one, his life was in danger when he was slandered "to the king" (51:6), and he believed himself to have had a narrow escape.

He is conscious of his own unusual attainments, and feels free to speak of them. The contrast between this unaffected pride of authorship and the impersonal manner of the canonical writers is very marked. The latter indeed, being ranked as "prophets" and represented as mouthpieces of the holy spirit, could claim no personal merit. Whether Bar Sira thought of himself as producing formal "prophecy" or not (24:33 is perhaps not to be pressed), it seems unlikely that either he or his readers can have thought of ranking his proverbs as holy scripture. The secular atmosphere of a considerable portion of the work sets it apart from the books of the sacred library.

In the religious teaching of Sirach there is nothing new or calling for especial attention. It is sometimes remarked that he makes no mention of the Messianic expectation, but the fact is hardly significant. One who had already been slandered to the Gentile monarch (see above) would not be inclined to speak plainly of a coming Jewish king. He does mention the forerunner Elijah in 48:10, quoting Mal. 3:23 f., and in 45:25 and 47:11 he implies an eternal covenant with David. In 36:1–10 his idea of the future of the Gentiles is like that which is consistently set forth in Isaiah, chapters 45, 49, 55, 60, and 66, and indeed in the later Hebrew writings generally: the inveterate enemies of

Israel and of Yahweh will be destroyed; the well-disposed nations (perhaps the great majority) will learn to know and serve Yahweh.

Sirach's proverbs are contained in chapters 1–42; and a poem, finely conceived and expressed, on the works of the Lord occupies 42:15–43:33. Then follows his famous eulogy of great men, 44:1–49:16. He praises in greater or less detail the fathers of Israel, presenting twenty-four of them by name, beginning with Enoch in 44:16 and ending with Nehemiah in 49:13. The Judges and Minor Prophets are mentioned as groups. (It is noticeable that as the representatives of the period of restoration he names Zerubbabel, Jeshua, and Nehemiah, ignoring Ezra, as is done also in the book of Enoch where the same three are named.) A supplementary paragraph adds mention of Enoch, Joseph, Shem, Seth, and Adam, for good measure. Finally, a special poem, 50:1–21, is devoted to the praise of the high priest Simon the son of Onias. This was Simon II, a contemporary of Sirach. The book ends with the autobiographical epilogue mentioned above, comprising 50:27–51:30. It consists of a brief introduction, a prayer, and an alphabetical acrostic poem, 51:13–30.

The proverbs are an impressive collection throughout, fully worthy of their author, who is a moralist of the first rank. They show a great variety, ranging from old Hebrew religious doctrine to practical maxims of every-day life and rules of etiquette such as 31:16 ff. and 32:4. The practical wisdom of 200 B.C. is not always that of the present day; this appears especially in the sections dealing with the family life. The personality of the author is also to be taken into account. Bar Sira lashes out so sharply at womankind that the conjecture has been natural that he had had some very unpleasant personal experience. A few examples of his bitter sayings are given in the General Introduction, §8. Nevertheless in a number of fine passages he gives glory to the wife of the family, and his praise of a happy marriage is most hearty.

The subjects treated are not arranged according to any recognizable plan, but seem to have been grouped as they came to mind. There is accordingly some repetition, hardly disturbing. Interest is well maintained, and the most hackneyed themes are likely to be given pungent expression. "Never repeat what is told you, and you will fare none the worse . . . . Have you heard a word? let it die with you; be of good courage, it will not burst you" (19:7, 10). "Seven days men mourn for the dead, but for a fool all the days of his life" (22:12). "The talk of a man of many oaths makes the hair stand on end" (27:14). "The stroke of a whip makes a mark in the flesh, but the stroke of a tongue breaks bones" (28:17).

Unfortunately, the translation often fails, and we are presented with mere nonsense in place of what was originally written. The grandson tells us in his prologue that he gave much toil and painstaking to the task of making his Greek version, and no one who studies his work will doubt that this was the case. But any translation of unpointed Hebrew into Greek is a difficult and precarious undertaking, and this version is full of errors, some of which are easily explained and corrected. Sirach's native tongue was doubtless Aramaic, and the language in which his book was composed was the classical Hebrew of the sacred books, to the study of which he had given much time and attention until he had gained "great familiarity with them," as his grandson informs us.

In and shortly after 1896 there came to light fragments of a Hebrew text of the book, the source of them being the *geniza* (storeroom) of a Cairo synagogue. Eventually they amounted to considerably more than half of the work.[89] These fragments were then hailed, and are now commonly accepted, as surviving portions of the original Hebrew text. There is strong reason for questioning this verdict. It is possible to see back of the Greek version a powerful and original Hebrew text, the work of a master of the literary language. In the Cairo Hebrew this impression is not maintained. What we read in a multitude of passages is commonplace, flabby, and distinctly second rate. It is customary to excuse much of this as "late Hebrew." The trouble is not with the character of the language, however, but with the lack of literary taste and skill. It is exactly what would be expected of a well-equipped writer of (say) the eighth or ninth century who should undertake, without any profound study, to reproduce the text of Ecclesiasticus, basing his work mainly on the Syriac version.[90] The question cannot be discussed here.

Literature. See §9.

89. The first publications: Cowley and Neubauer, *The Original Hebrew of a Portion of Ecclesiasticus,* 39:15–49:11 (Oxford, 1897); Schechter and Taylor, *The Wisdom of Ben Sira* (Cambridge, 1899). The most convenient publication of the principal fragments: H. L. Strack, *Die Sprüche Jesus', des Sohnes Sirachs* (Leipzig, 1903), with notes and vocabulary.

90. Many Hebrew and Aramaic texts of the book must have been produced from time to time after the original had perished; at first from memory, afterwards from the existing versions; this in spite of the curious prohibition of the book by Rabbi Akiba, recorded in the Talmud (Jer. Sanhedrin, x, 1, fol. 28a); see Section 3 in the General Introduction.

§23. The Wisdom of Solomon

This book, which in some respects represents the high-water mark in the apocryphal literature, bore from the first the name "The Wisdom of Solomon"; but it was also entitled "The Book of Wisdom," or simply "Wisdom." Thus in both ancient and modern times. It is unique among the extra-canonical Jewish theological writings in the clear impression which it gives of an Alexandrian Greek origin.

It must be said at the outset, before beginning to characterize the book in detail, that it is a composite work consisting of two nearly equal halves. The first half was originally a Hebrew poetical composition, given out in the name of the king of Israel, the son of David; the second half is Alexandrian religious philosophy, composed in the rhetorical Greek of the later Ptolemaic period. The author of the second half translated the first half into Greek, and made it the introduction to his own elaborate composition.

The author of the Hebraic division of the book speaks plainly and frequently in the character of King Solomon; see 7:1–8; 8:9–11; 9:7, 8, 12. In this use of the pseudonym there can have been no thought of deception. The name was already familiar as representative of this whole class of Jewish literature, and it was recognized as a convenient disguise to be used in a "wisdom" writing which assumed a tone of authority, the writer thus indicating that he preferred to remain anonymous. In the present case the fiction of the royal speaker is clearly in place, for the instruction is addressed to "princes" and "judges of the earth"; see 6: 1–4, 9–11. The book begins with a similar address, 1:1, though from this point on to the end of chapter 5 there is nothing to suggest either Solomon or an audience of magnates.

The first section of the book, chapters 1–5, is a powerful statement of the writer's religious philosophy, and is generally regarded as the finest fruit of the Jewish theology of its time. It is largely taken up with a contrast drawn between the lot of the righteous man and that of his ungodly opponent, not so much in this life as in the life after death. The emphasis throughout the section is on eschatology, and the writer's teaching of the doctrine of immortality has been famous from the earliest times, especially the passage beginning: "The souls of the righteous are in the hand of God, and no torment shall touch them" (3:1). The chief opponents of the good man, in the mind of the writer, are evidently the renegades from Judaism, see especially 2:12b, 14. There is to be a state of future retribution for the wicked; but it is not clear, even from 4:18–20,[91] what conception of it the author held.

91. Vs. 20 sounds like one of the embellishments of the second author.

The praise of Wisdom begins at once, in 1:4, 6, and is continued throughout the first half of the book, being never lost from sight. Wisdom is life, and the guide to eternal life; whoever possesses her is near to God. She was with God when he created the world (9:9). When the first man transgressed, she stood by him and "delivered him from *mortal* sin" (10:1, see Purinton, pp. 294 f.). In chapters 6–9 the true nature of Wisdom is set forth, the blessings she brings, and how she may be attained. Her work is to be seen in all that is great and beautiful. She must be held in honor and eagerly sought. "I called upon God," says Solomon, "and there came to me a spirit of wisdom" (7:7). His experience of wisdom is set forth at some length, and the words of his prayer are given in chapter 9.

In chapter 10 the author begins to show how Wisdom has been the true guide and savior of mankind from Adam onward. Abraham is introduced in 10:5, and thereafter the wonderful deliverance of Israel from distress and danger is rapidly sketched, up to the time of the wandering in the desert after the flight from Egypt. A holy prophet, Moses, was the leader, but Wisdom was his guide (11:1). From this point to the end of the book, 19:22, there is no mention of wisdom.

In the earlier part of the book little attention was paid to the foreign peoples, for the writer's chief concern was with individuals, with the godly man and his ungodly associates. With chapter 10 there is introduced the familiar antithesis between the chosen people and the Gentiles, between the righteous nation and its determined foes. Joseph held the scepter of authority over those who had been his tyrants and accusers. "Wisdom delivered a holy people and a blameless seed from a nation of oppressors" (vs. 15). The depths of the Red Sea were a highway for Israel, but a grave for the Egyptians (18 f.). Here is brought into view the theme to which the *second* writer is so passionately devoted, the superiority of Israel to its wealthy and powerful neighbors who now have the upper hand. It may be conjectured that the opportunity here given to the latter author by this fine poem addressed to kings and princes was what led him to translate it and to continue with his own forceful invective which fills the next nine chapters.

The second half of the book is a polemic against the Gentiles. It is usually the Egyptians who are mentioned or kept in mind, and the writer accordingly deals, first and last, with the sojourn of the Israelites in the land of bondage in the days of Moses and Aaron, and with the plagues which were brought upon the wicked and malevolent people. The tone of bitter enmity which is sometimes heard in this second part of the book, and is remarked upon by all commentators, is perhaps more a literary property than the expression of the writer's personal feeling. Even so, it would be difficult to believe this author to be the same as the one who wrote the first half.

The greater portion of the work which now follows is constructed on a fanciful scheme which is partly stated at the outset, in 11:5:[92] "By what things their foes were punished, by these they in their need were benefited." Thus, instead of the fountains of fresh water which flowed for the Israelites, the rivers of the thirsting Egyptians were turned into blood, in punishment for their decree to slay the Hebrew babies. Another feature of the "scheme" is stated in verse 16, the punishment fits the crime: "By what things a man sinneth, by these he is punished." The two principles are accordingly demonstrated at considerable length in the case of each of the plagues of Egypt—not without an amount of forced interpretation. Also, the Egyptians worshiped animals and reptiles (11:15), wherefore fearful beasts, hideous creatures, and vermin were sent upon them (11:17 ff., 16:1), while to the Israelites quails "of rare taste" were sent.

Attention is paid to the Canaanites, their sin and punishment, and the extent to which they were spared, in 12:3–11; and in 13:1–15:17 there is a long digression, a tirade against idolatry.

The literary style in this second half of the book is generally inflated and bombastic, very different from that in the first ten chapters. In both thought and diction there are marked differences between the two halves, as Holmes, in Charles's *Apocrypha*, has well shown. The main literary characteristics of a writer are notably stable, and it seems a necessary conclusion that the book is the work of two authors.

The question of the original language, or languages, is more than usually interesting because of the character of the work. For a long time it was taken for granted that it was composed in Greek throughout. The prevailing element of Alexandrian philosophy, and the florid Greek rhetoric so conspicuous in the latter chapters, seemed to give a plain answer. The diction of the same learned Greek scholar, moreover, is unmistakably present in every part.[93] The question appeared to be settled.

As early as the middle of the 18th century, however, the verdict in favor of Greek as the original language of the whole was strongly

92. Possibly the work of the second author began at just this point instead of at vs. 2, in which case he must be supposed to have discarded the original ending of the poem, as standing in the way of his present purpose. On the other hand, as one thoroughly versed in the Greek Bible he would naturally write balanced clauses in the Hebrew manner where the subject gave the impulse. Whoever wrote vss. 2–4 had in memory Ps. 107:4–6 and Deut. 8:15. The wording here does not suggest the LXX version of the psalm.

93. See Swete, *Introduction to the Old Testament in Greek*, pp. 311 f.

attacked. The remarkable change in the literary structure, after the earlier part of the book, was especially called to attention, the regular parallelism at the beginning indicating translation from Hebrew. Other evidence was added: Solomon, who is the speaker in the first nine chapters, is not again mentioned; Wisdom, dominating the first ten chapters, disappears with Solomon. Scholars in increasing number argued for a composite work: in the first half, Hebrew poetry; in the second half, Greek rhetoric of the Alexandrian type, the writer making a half-hearted attempt to continue the parallelism, as though despising the cheap device but compelled to use it to some extent. There was disagreement as to the point where the second author comes in, and a wish for more definite evidence of translation.

Quite recently, two American scholars, E. A. Speiser and C. E. Purinton (see Literature), have taken up anew the question, aiming especially to demonstrate mistranslation in the Greek; a difficult and precarious line of proof, but of the first importance. Probably few qualified judges who examine the evidence now produced in 1:14; 8:4; 9:1; 10:1, and 10:10, viewed in the light of all the evidence of a composite work, will hesitate to accept the verdict of an originally Hebrew first division of the book. As to the extent of this portion, Purinton's conclusion, which is that of Holmes (see above) and of some earlier scholars, that the second author began his own composition just after the beginning of chapter 11, seems well established.

Some difficulties remain. Cornill, *Einleitung* (1896), p. 278, remarks that such a passage as 7:22 f., with its enumeration of twenty-one qualities and characteristics of Wisdom, would be quite anomalous in Hebrew (especially, he might have added, in Hebrew poetry). The objection is valid, and there are other portions of this seventh chapter which give evidence of expansion by the second author. Swete, *Introduction*, p. 269, gives a list of twenty-three unusual Greek words found in the book. It seems worth while to note that of these, eleven occur only in the second half; *nine* are found in chapter 7 (two of them elsewhere in the first half); four occur in chapter 4. The repetitious style of the second author seems quite evident in 7:22b–26, in which passage *seven* of the "unusual words" mentioned above are found, while the Hebrew parallelism is not maintained. It seems clear that the translator, who was also editor and author, felt free to embellish the document which he supplemented.

Recognition of Wisdom 1–10 as originally Hebrew does not imply its Palestinian origin. It is true that we know very little about the literary Palestine of this time, and it is possible that Greek philosophy was sufficiently familiar there to make natural such a publication as this. On the other hand, there were of course Jewish scholars in Egypt who could write elegant Hebrew, and every hint that is given either by the mode of thought or by the apparent circumstances of the author points to Egypt.

Wherever the first half of the book was composed, it is a notable landmark in the history of religious thought. Its author may have had no idea of producing anything new, he wrote what he and his fellows believed. The doctrines which had been developed in the Greek world were not foreign to Israelite theology, but were helpful to it. He himself had read widely, perhaps not deeply, in Hellenic philosophy, and was conscious of the gain from it. The modified Judaism of the "school" to which he belonged has in it much that is strikingly like what we see in the earliest Christian writers; and this is true also of the second half of the book, the work of his interpreter and successor.

He holds the loyal Jew's view of the Scriptures and the Mosaic law, though when he declares the superiority of Israel to all other peoples he grounds it in knowledge of God rather than of the Torah. He is not concerned with the Gentiles, except to glean incidentally from their wisdom. He shows the influence of Plato, perhaps directly in 9:15, and deals with standard Greek philosophy in 8:7 (the four "cardinal virtues") and in 7:24, 27 and 8:1. Out of his freer type of theology come numerous ideas which, while plainly resting on doctrines of the canonical scriptures, yet occupy new ground. It may be taken for granted that the second author shared the views of his predecessor. An interesting minor item is the identification of the serpent of Eden with the Devil, which appears here for the first time in literature (2:24; cf. Rev. 12:9 and 20:2). It is noticeable that there is in the book no allusion to the Messianic hope, a fact which certainly suggests that the authors wrote in one of the lands of the Dispersion rather than in Palestine.

Regarding the use of the book of Wisdom in the New Testament, see the General Introduction, the section dealing with such use of the extra-canonical literature.

The question of the date has been variously answered, always with hesitation, for there is nothing in the contents of the book that could give a definite clue, and this is true also of its literary relations. Guesses ranging from 150 B.C. to A.D. 40 have been made. The former of the two dates may seem too early, yet there is no apparent reason why it is necessary to go much later. The doctrines of the book are not new because they embody late conceptions, but because they fuse Jewish orthodoxy with Greek ideas of long standing. What seems a truly important clue is furnished by Thackeray in his *Grammar* (1909), pp. 58–62. On the basis of a thoroughly studied literary usage he would assign the Greek text to the period 132–100 B.C.

Holmes (see above), pp. 520 f., argues from a supposed use of LXX Proverbs (dated by Thackeray about 100 B.C.) by the translator of Wisdom; but it is difficult to see, after a close examination of the passages named, any adequate basis for the supposition.[94] The impersonation of Wisdom makes certain ideas and phrases inevitable, and the corresponding Hebrew words have their standing Greek equivalents. The last quarter of the 2d century B.C. seems the probable date for the completed work.

Literature. See §9; also F. C. Porter, "The Pre-existence of the Soul in the Book of Wisdom," in *Old Testament and Semitic Studies in Memory of W. R. Harper,* I (1907), 207–269. E. A. Speiser, "The Hebrew Origin of the First Part of the Book of Wisdom," *Jewish Quarterly Rev.* (April, 1924). C. E. Purinton, "Translation Greek in the Wisdom of Solomon," *Jour. Bib. Lit., 47* (1928), 276–304.

§24. FOURTH MACCABEES

THIS is a work of homiletical character, more exactly a diatribe of the Greek pattern, deriving the most of its illustrative material from the story of the Jewish martyrs told in 2 Macc. 6:18–7:42. It also has in part the form of a philosophical treatise with a subject definitely stated at the outset: the author will show that "the pious reason is absolute master of the passions" (1:1, see also vs. 13; 18:2, etc.). The book therefore appears at an early date with the superscription περὶ αὐτοκράτορος λογισμοῦ, "On the Supreme Power of Reason" (thus in Eusebius and Jerome). The title "Fourth Maccabees" is also attested very early.

In a brief introductory passage the author indicates the scope of the question, and the nature of the chief illustration which he will use (1:1–11). He then states in a single sentence (1:12) the plan of his discourse: first, a philosophical discussion of the main proposition; then the illustration afforded by the history of the Maccabean martyrs. The book has thus two main divisions: 1. The philosophical discussion (1:13–3:18); 2. the story of the martyrs, with the lessons to be learned from it (3:19–end). This second division is based on Second Maccabees, chapters 3–7.

The discourse on the sufferings and triumph of the Jewish martyrs,

94. Holmes's argument from Wisd. 6:14 is particularly unfortunate. The two passages (duplicates) in Proverbs are both secondary and out of place, and it is easy to see the origin of each of them. The δυναστῶν in 8:3 is a duplicate rendering of the second Hebrew word in vs. 2; the *verb* was very possibly suggested by the word employed in Wisd. 6:14 and 9:4.

which constitutes three-fourths of the whole book, begins with chapter 5. Its framework is an expanded version of 2 Macc. 6:18–7:42. The following divisions are more or less distinctly marked: Narrative of the trial and torture of the aged priest Eleazar (5:1–6:30). Lessons drawn from this narrative (6:31–7:23). Description of the torture of the seven youths (8:1–12:19). Comments on their fortitude (13:1–14:10). Reflections on the sufferings and the constancy of the mother (14:11–17:6). Conclusion (17:7–18:23).

The book is a fine example of the way in which a treatise in Hebrew theology could wear with ease and grace a dress made in the Greek schools. It represents Hellenistic culture of the best type. Its author consciously assumes the attitude of a champion of the study of philosophy (1:1), and it is plain that he wishes to make prominent the philosophical side of his discourse, though aiming primarily to give religious instruction. See 5:6–11, 7:18, etc. The prevailingly Stoic coloring of his philosophy is to be noticed; see the "four cardinal virtues" in 1:18, and compare 1:2–6; 2:23; 5:22 f.; and 15:7. It is quite plain, however, that Fourth Maccabees represents no particular school; nor does its author appear as the advocate of any "system" made up from Greek and Jewish elements; his philosophy is merely a part of his general culture.

The religion which the book preaches is Judaism through and through, somewhat enriched from Greek thought, but nonetheless loyal to the faith of the fathers. The preacher will inspire his hearers by the example of the constancy and devotion of the heroes of the great persecution. In drawing the lesson he displays the most ardent patriotism, and zeal for the ceremonial law. The motive that actuated these heroes was not so much the hope of gaining eternal life as the steadfast purpose to perform their duty (12:12, cf. 5:16 ff., 6:14 ff., etc.). They died in obedience to God, in support of the law, in behalf of a cause. By their death they wrought deliverance for their nation.

In this connection the writer gives expression to a doctrine which is one of the most interesting features of the book on the side of its theology, namely, the belief that the death of a martyr is in some way an expiatory offering in behalf of his people (6:29; 17:21; cf. 2 Macc. 7:37 f.). The eschatology of the book is also of especial interest. The doctrine of the immortality of the soul is of course made prominent; but what is emphasized by the writer is not the belief in the resurrection of the dead, as in Second Maccabees, but rather the doctrine that all souls, whether righteous or wicked, exist forever after death. The good will be in eternal happiness, with the fathers of Israel and with God; the wicked will be in torment, burning in everlasting fire.

The personal earnestness and enthusiasm of the writer are manifest at every point. He is a true preacher, not a mere rhetorician, and his discourse is something very different from a formal exercise. It is evident from the manner and tone of the whole composition that the aim of its author was less to gain intellectual assent to a proposition than to give a religious impulse. He shows himself thoroughly acquainted with the Hebrew scriptures, and he assumes that his hearers are. The reference in 18:8 to the serpent, *the evil spirit*, of Genesis 3 (compare Wisd. 2:24) is to be noticed, and so also is the expression "the rib that was built up," referring to the story of Eve, in 18:7. The whole passage 18:6 ff. gives us a very interesting glimpse of Jewish family life of the writer's own day.

In form and content the Greek diatribe has more or less distinctly the appearance of a speaker's address to his audience. This appearance is consistently maintained in Fourth Maccabees. In the opening words the author speaks of himself in the first person and of his hearers in the second person, and he continues to do this in the sequel. In 18:1 he addresses his hearers, "men of Israel," in the vocative. Rhetorical devices and turns of expression such as belong properly to an oration are frequent. In the words of 1:12, "I will now speak . . . as I have been wont to do," the author represents himself as preaching to his accustomed audience. The modern reader, aware of the gain from the preacher's own presence in oral delivery, is tempted to see in such earnest diatribes as this (the N. T. Epistle to the Hebrews is a similar example) real sermons uttered in synagogue or church. There is no impossibility in the supposition of such Jewish-Greek homilies uttered in person, but proof is wanting.

The literary skill and taste shown by the writer of Fourth Maccabees deserve in the main high praise. He writes with dignity, and with an evident consciousness of mastery. The rhetorical power which he exhibits is very considerable. The one great blemish in the book from the modern point of view is its detailed description (exaggerated beyond the bounds of reason) of the tortures to which the martyrs were subjected. Such descriptions were in demand at that day, and there are many examples of the kind in the early Christian literature, but they are quite intolerable now.

As a specimen of Hellenistic Greek the book has always received high praise. Jerome says of it (*De viris illustr.*, 13)[95] *valde elegans habetur,* and with this the modern verdict agrees. The style is well suited to the matter, simple in the narrative portions and rhetorical where this quality is in place. It is smooth flowing and vigorous, always well finished and rarely overloaded. Well constructed periods

95. This is in his treatment of Josephus, to whom (for no good reason) the authorship of Fourth Maccabees had been attributed.

abound. In the use of classical constructions (for example, the optative mood) the writer stands almost alone among Jewish-Greek authors. His style and diction do not appear to have been influenced by the LXX, though he occasionally quotes from it. Hebraisms are almost totally wanting.

The author must have composed his diatribe in some city where the Jews were for the most part completely Hellenized. The most probable place, beyond doubt, is Alexandria, but there are other possibilities. The question of the date is wide open, the only certainty being that the book is later than Second Maccabees. A time early in the last century B.C. is perhaps as good a guess as any other.

Literature. See §9; also Freudenthal, *Die Flavius Josephus beigelegte Schrift . . . eine Predigt aus dem ersten nachchristlichen Jahrhundert* (1869).

§25. The Psalms of Solomon

THE eighteen "Psalms of Solomon" are mentioned in some of the early church lists of the sacred books, and they have been given numerous editions, from 1626 to recent times. Especially convenient for English readers is the edition by H. E. Ryle and M. R. James, Greek text and English translation (Cambridge, 1891). In this publication they were given the sub-title "Psalms of the Pharisees." The Greek text is printed in Swete's LXX, III, 765–787.

The original language of the psalms was Hebrew, as is now generally understood, but they have been preserved only in Greek (several manuscripts). There is some evidence that a Latin translation, presumably made from the Greek, was once in existence. No record or trace of any other ancient version was known until the discovery of the Syriac version, made from the Greek, which was first published by J. Rendel Harris in his *Odes and Psalms of Solomon* (Cambridge, 1909).

These psalms in their literary character and form are in all respects like those of the Psalter. The most of them have superscriptions (probably translated from the Hebrew), and the Greek rendering of the familiar "*selah*" occurs twice, in 17:31 and 18:10, testifying to the fact of a regular liturgical use. Why they were ascribed to Solomon is a matter for conjecture; perhaps it was merely in order to give them a convenient label of early date. Where they deal with the conventional themes of the Hebrew psalmists—and this is the case with the most of them—they bring nothing new and are not impressive. (In judging of their literary quality it is necessary to remember that the original Hebrew has perished, and that the Greek is often faulty.)

There is one respect, however, in which their contribution to early Jewish literature is both interesting and important. The hymns of the canonical Hebrew Psalter are characteristically timeless; hints as to political conditions giving ground for a definite dating are hardly to be found. Several of the Psalms of Solomon, on the contrary, were brought forth directly by the political situation in Jerusalem, and throw a strong light on the prevailing temper in orthodox circles under the conditions described.

There has been a party in power which has misused its high office and brought great harm to the state, usurping unlawful prerogatives including even the Kingship (17:5–8). Lawless themselves, these malefactors have filled the land with wickedness. Here, as most interpreters agree, it is plain that the late Hasmonean princes are meant. They have at least met with their just deserts (vs. 10), for a foreign conqueror has taken the city and has slain or exiled these evil-doers (vs. 14). As for the pagan conqueror himself, he and all his kind must be driven out (vss. 23–27):

Behold, Lord, and raise up for thy people their king, the son of David,
At the time which thou, God, hast appointed, to hold sway over Israel, thy servant.
Gird him with strength to shatter the wicked rulers,
Cleansing Jerusalem from the Gentiles who trample it to destruction;
In wisdom and righteousness to drive out the evil men from our inheritance,
Crushing their arrogance like the vessels of the potter,
Shattering all their substance with a rod of iron,
Destroying the ungodly nations with the word of his mouth.

Such an outburst of national feeling as this, calling for rebellion under a native king and expulsion of the foreign oppressors, would ordinarily spell danger to the speaker and to his people (cf. John 11:47 f.). The uprising of the Maccabees had been a sufficient lesson. "King" was a term generally avoided; Daniel's "man" ("Son of Man") was far safer and widely used. Were the immediate circumstances such that a fiery exhortation to sedition could be made with comparative safety?

We know who this foreign tyrant was. He who came from the west, who razed certain parts of the city wall with a battering-ram (2:1), after being welcomed by a certain party of Jewish leaders (8:18–24);

he who sent his royal captives (Aristobulus II and his family) to
Rome, as is mentioned in 17:14, was Pompey, who invaded Palestine
in 63 B.C. He had already met his end when the second psalm of this
group was written, see 2:30 f.: "I had not long to wait before God
showed me the insolent one slain on the mountains(?) of Egypt,
. . . his body borne hither and thither on the waves, with no one to
bury him." This was actually Pompey's fate, in 48 B.C., and the
psalm must have been written very soon after that date. It is possible
that all the poems of the little collection are the work of one author,
for the tone is the same throughout, and there is no clear evidence of
any very different date.

The picture of the Davidic king, the Messiah, which was begun in
the 17th psalm in the lines above quoted, is continued there in lines
27–49, and is still further elaborated in 18:6–10. Here, as everywhere
else, he is a divine being. He will smite the earth with the word of his
mouth forever (39), cf. Is. 11:4 and 2 Esd. 13:10; He is taught of
God (35); the right-minded Gentile nations will be holy in his days
(35, 36), cf. Is. 66:21; God will be his king (38); he will tend God's
flock with faith and righteousness (45).

It is obvious that the poet is here dealing with long-familiar ideas
and expressions. He and his readers held the same doctrine which is
set forth in Enoch, the same in all particulars as that which was
enounced by Second Isaiah more than three centuries earlier. This
teaching concerning the Messiah, here not given obscurely but brought
out into the open, and by rare good fortune preserved, is the most
valuable feature of these hymns.

The striking resemblance of Psalms of Solomon 11 to Bar. 4:36–5:9
has long been noticed, and in recent years the view has prevailed that
Baruch was the borrower. In the section here dealing with the book of
Baruch the contrary view is maintained, for the original language was
not Greek, but Hebrew, and the date comparatively early.

Literature. See §9; also the edition of Ryle and James, mentioned above; it
has valuable notes and a full Introduction. J. Rendel Harris and A. Mingana,
The Odes and Psalms of Solomon, 2 vols. (Manchester, 1916, 1920).

§26. THE SIBYLLINE BOOKS

COLLECTIONS of Sibylline oracles had exercised considerable influence
in pagan lands long before the beginning of the present era. The divinely inspired Sibyl could impart wisdom to men, or to peoples,
making known to them the will of the gods and showing them what
course to take in any great emergency. The oracles were given their

typical form in Greek surroundings, and the various collections continued to be written in hexameter verse.

Prophetesses of this type were celebrated in various places, from Babylonia to Italy. Especially renowned was the Erythraean sibyl in Ionia. The Cumaean sibyl and her books, familiar from Vergil and from the story of Tarquinius Priscus (otherwise T. Superbus) played a very important part in early Roman history. Her oracles, in charge of the decemvirs and frequently consulted, were destroyed in the burning of the temple of Jupiter in 83 B.C. A new book of oracles, obtained chiefly in Ionia, was soon in use, but this also eventually perished.

In the meantime a sibylline collection of growing importance had been taking shape in Egypt, and during much of its early history it was strongly under the influence of the Roman oracles just mentioned. The Jews of Alexandria began at an early date to make skillful use of "the Sibyl" for their propaganda. Beginning with a strong nucleus of pagan oracles, it was possible through interpolation and gradual expansion to introduce monotheism, the Mosaic ordinances, and important features of the Hebrew history of mankind. The Gentiles would listen gladly to the inspired hexameters, which contained much of their own histories and some of their mythology. The sibylline teaching was in favor everywhere. One important standing feature of all this literature, from the earliest time, had been the "prophecy after the event," the prophetess narrating in detail the successive chapters of history in the form of a prediction made long beforehand. The pagan sibyl, of whatever land, was understood to be the sister (or daughter) of Apollo. The Egyptian sibyl of the Jewish undertaking, introducing herself as the daughter-in-law of Noah (III, 827), had a clear field from the deluge onward. In line 809 she tells of having taken up her abode in Babylonia.

When the Jews had finished with their undertaking, the Christians took it up and carried it on until about the 6th century A.D. The entire work comprised fifteen books, of which twelve are now known to be in existence, Books IX, X, and XV being still missing. Evidence has been set forth to show that a considerable part of Book III was composed in the middle of the 2d century B.C., in the reign of Ptolemy VII. Books IV and V also are of Jewish origin, with some Christian interpolation, and it is probable that both were composed in Egypt. These three are the only sibylline books of which any notice need be taken in a work dealing with the O. T. apocrypha, and their importance is very slight. In my *Documents of the Primitive Church*, pp. 234 f., it was shown that both IV, which seems to have been finished at about the year 80, and V, which was completed in the second century, appear to make use of the N. T. Revelation.

The Third Book, the longest of the three, is a chaos, but it is well fitted to give an idea of the plan conceived by the Jews of Egypt and the manner of its execution. Some purely pagan oracles are here given a new edition. There are woes on various lands. In 167, after an impressive Introduction, the Sibyl begins a sketch of universal history, and in 171–284 the Hebrews and their religion are glorified, with especial attention given to Moses and the law in 252–260. The Messianic time is predicted in 741–761, 767–795. The material of the Book is of various dates (see above) ; the passages mentioning Beliar, 63–74, and the widow (Rome) ruling over the whole world, 77, are of the Christian era.

Contemporary Roman history plays a conspicuous part in each of the other two books, and gives help in dating. The Fourth Book, in 130 ff., mentions the great eruption of Vesuvius in A.D. 79. The Fifth Book, in 397–413, bewails the devastation wrought by the armies of Titus; but in 48 f. warmly praises Hadrian (A.D. 117–138), thus assuring a date in the early part of his reign, before the disastrous war. Line 51 certainly appears to be secondary.

Literature. See §9; also the editions of the Greek text by Rzach (1891), and Geffcken (1902), with a valuable Introduction. The English translation in Charles's *Apocrypha,* Vol. II, is by H. C. O. Lanchester.

§27. ENOCH

THE book of Enoch, the only one of the apocryphal books to be directly quoted in the New Testament (Jude 14), is the best typical example of an apocalypse. Both in its extent and in the variety of its material it surpasses all the other works of its class. The patriarch Enoch was naturally suggested by Gen. 5:24 as the recipient of special revelations. Not all those attributed to him are contained in this book,[96] and on the other hand some of the material included here was not in the original edition. While mainly the work of one author, it has received accretions of its own type. Imagination is a chief characteristic of the Hebrew writers in general, and this quality has striking illustration in the work before us.

The Semitic (Aramaic) original has perished, and only a small part of the Greek translation has been preserved. For a complete text of the book we are confined to the Ethiopic version, which was made from the Greek.

96. There is especially to be mentioned the *Book of the Secrets of Enoch,* published by W. R. Morfill and R. H. Charles in 1896. This is a book originally composed in Greek but now extant only in a Slavonic version. It is based throughout on our apocalypse, but contains some new material and is completely refashioned. It is not clear that it is of Jewish origin, nor that the claim of an early date is justified.

There is a brief introduction, chapters 1–5, in which Enoch announces himself and gives in general terms a summary of his religious instruction designed for "the remote generations to come." Chapters 6–36 are taken up with the highly developed angelology which is characteristic of the book and found in every part of it: the sinning angels of Gen. 6:1–4 and their offspring; the punishment meted out to them and reserved for them; the holy angels; the travels of the seer, conducted by some of them, to the ends of the earth.

Chapters 37–71 constitute a clearly marked-off division of the book. It is given its own title in 37:5, "The Discourses." These are three in number: chapters 38–44, dealing chiefly with the secrets of the heavens; 45–57, treating mainly of the Messiah, but also (in its latter part) of the punishment of the fallen angels; 58–69, a discourse concerning the righteous and the elect, the judgment pronounced on the wicked, the orders of the angels. The most important part of this division of the book is the teaching as to the Son of Man, the Elect One. This indeed contains nothing new; it is the very same doctrine which had been proclaimed in the Hebrew scriptures and taken for granted by all the Jews for two or three centuries past;[97] the unique circumstance is its formulation in some detail as part of a theological treatise.

Chapters 72–82 occupy a place by themselves, for they deal with astronomy and physics, particularly with the laws of the heavenly bodies and the chronological system obtained from them. Enoch's 365 years (Gen. 5:23) designated him as especially interested in the calendar. This section of the book is an interesting monument of the learning and of the curious scientific notions of the Judaism of its day.

In chapters 83–90 Enoch tells his son Methuselah of two especially portentous dream-visions which he had seen. The first of these was the announcement to him of the destruction of mankind by the deluge. The second, in some respects the most important feature of the whole book, is a conspectus of human history from the beginning to the author's own day in the parable of the bulls, the sheep, and the shepherds, this occupying chapters 85–90. Those details of the vision from which the date of the book can be inferred will be discussed below.

Among the other features there are two which may be mentioned as interesting. The three "builders" after the destruction of Jerusalem by the Chaldeans (89:72) are Zerubbabel, Jeshua, and Nehemiah. Ezra is ignored here, just as he is passed over in Sirach 49:11–13, where also the three are Zerubbabel, Jeshua, and Nehemiah. At the end of the vision, in 90:37, 38, it seems evident that the *two* Messiahs, well known to the Jewish eschatology of the last centuries B.C., are

97. Inability to recognize this fact has been the most serious failure of modern Biblical theology. See *Our Translated Gospels*, pp. xv–xxviii, where the evidence is set forth.

pictured. The white bull with great horns is the Messiah son of David; the wild-ox with great black horns (Deut. 33:17) is the other Messiah, the son of Joseph and Ephraim. See the *Jour. Am. Or. Soc., 62* (1942), 57.

Chapters 91–108, containing the religious instruction given by Enoch to his assembled children, deal mainly with eschatology. There is good evidence that chapter 105 (consisting of only two verses) is a later insertion; it seems ill suited to its context, and is wanting in the Greek.[98] Chapters 106 and 107, dealing with the birth of Noah, seem out of place. Chapter 108, professedly "another book which Enoch wrote for his son Methuselah," is evidently secondary, for it is not found in the Greek.

The question of secondary elements in the great apocalypse is difficult. There are doubtless many *minor* accretions, not always to be recognized with certainty. The important section of the three Discourses, chapters 37–71, has frequently been pronounced a later addition to the original work, but hardly on sufficient grounds. Chapters 65–69(?), in which Noah is the speaker, have been supposed to come from a "lost Apocalypse of Noah," and a few other passages have been conjectured to have the same origin, but there is no clear evidence of any such work. No writer dealing so constantly with the deluge and with the wickedness which brought it on the earth could fail to introduce the righteous great-grandson of Enoch at some point, and imagination would naturally produce the lively pictures which we see. The allusions to Noah's written wisdom in Jub. 10:10–14 and 21:10 are no evidence of a lost book! Chapters 106 f., mentioned above, seem from their position to be secondary.

The book makes decidedly the impression of a late work, the time of the Maccabean struggle seems long past. The date of the main body of the work is provided in the vision of the bulls and sheep, chapters 85–90, which presents in figurative language the history of the Israelite world from Adam to the dawn of the Messianic age. Seventy "shepherds," angels, were appointed to have charge of the chosen people (89:56), and the whole history is divided into seventy "times" consisting of four definite periods disposed as follows. To each of the first and fourth periods twelve times and twelve shepherds (the sacred number) are assigned; the two middle periods are equal, each covering twenty-three times, thus completing the number seventy.

The first period, of 12, extends from Adam to Cyrus; the second period, of 23, from Cyrus to Alexander; the third period, of 23, from

98. Chaps. 97–107 were edited from recently discovered Greek papyri by Campbell Bonner in *The Last Chapters of Enoch in Greek* (London, 1937). Chaps. 1–32 had been known in Greek since 1892.

Alexander to the Maccabees; the fourth period, of 12, to the end of the present age. Thus in 89:72–90:17.

The sheep represent the Israelites, the lambs born of white sheep are the Maccabees, and the horns which at length appear can only represent the Hasmonean *priest-kings*, their power culminating in the "great horn" (90:9) symbolizing John Hyrcanus. So the most of the interpreters, from Ewald and Dillmann onward, have decided. The historical sketch is so summary here as to include only what its author absolutely required. Mattathias is not symbolized at all, and Judas has mention (as "one of the lambs") only in verse 8.[99] Charles has attempted to show, both in his Commentary and elsewhere, that the "great horn" is Judas. Verse 9, with its "horns" *preceding* the chief one, seems quite conclusive against this interpretation, and sufficiently clear in its indication that the horn symbolizes *the world power* which the Jews held in the persons of Jonathan and his successors. At first, "the ravens cast down the horns" (vs. 9), referring to the fact that Jonathan and Simon, successively, were captured and put to death by the "ravens". It was under Hyrcanus that the Jewish state reached the zenith of its national renown, and verse 12 tells of his glorious reign. "The nation was in complete accord with its leader" (Wellhausen, *Isr. u. jüd. Geschichte,*[5] p. 281).

The period in Enoch's vision does not end in glory, however, and the fact must not be overlooked. Verses 13–16 tell of distress which soon came, in spite of help given by the archangel Michael (vs. 14). Verse 13 introduces a new actor, as the formula, "And I saw," etc., indicates; the birds of prey now come together in the attempt "to break the horn of *a certain* ram" (on the demonstrative pronoun here see Dalman, *Grammar,* 113 f.). This is not Judas Aristobulus, whose reign of only one year could not deserve notice here, the allusion is to the disastrous reign of Hyrcanus' second son, Alexander Jannaeus (102–76). His many and bloody wars were a grievous burden, he himself was cordially hated from the first, and he made the Pharisees his bitter enemy.[100]

Verse 16 is the immediate continuation of 14. Verse 15 was introduced too soon by a scribe whose eye, as he finished writing verse 14,

99. The supposed reference here to the high priest Onias III does not suit vs. 8, which plainly implies the death of a military leader. Onias was murdered in cold blood by the instigation of the renegade high priest Menelaus. He was not a man of great influence, and his death was of very slight historical importance. The supposition that his fate is referred to in Dan. 9:25 is also mistaken, as will be shown elsewhere.

100. The foolish story told in Josephus, *Antt.,* 13, x, 5, 6, and repeated in the Talmud, of a break with the Pharisees in the latter years of Hyrcanus, deserves not a particle of credence; as Schürer remarks, it bears the stamp of legend, and all the known facts prove it false. Whoever devised it wished to show that the Pharisees had openly questioned the authority of the Hasmonean priesthood even in the case of the Great Hyrcanus.

happened to fall on the very similar verse 17, whereupon he continued with its sequel (now vs. 15) which told of the wrath of the Lord of the sheep and the flight of the guilty angels (shepherds) into the darkness.

These verses are evidently important for the dating of the book. Michael comes down in answer to a cry and gives his help; this can only refer to a signal victory which had been delayed. But Michael finds the conditions in Israel so bad that his gloomy report brings on the end of the world. It is worthy of notice that Jannaeus' most important conquest, that of the Phoenician cities ending with the capture of Gaza *after a siege lasting a year*, took place in 96 B.C.; and that immediately thereafter he was waging war with an army of mercenaries against his own people, a civil war in which tens of thousands of the Jews perished. Here, apparently, is new light thrown on verses 14 and 17. An especially sinister fact was the wholesale butchery of the Pharisees (Josephus, *Antt.*, 13, xiii, 5), which the interpreters of Enoch rightly find referred to in 47:1–4. This certainly was a time to look for the speedy coming of the Messiah!

The book is thus to be dated in the first decade of the last century B.C., *probably* in or soon after the year 95. No part of the book appears to be earlier than this.

For the original language of the book, Greek was at first taken for granted. Eventually it was made clear by one scholar after another that the Greek is a translation, and a Hebrew Enoch was naturally conjectured. It was soon seen that the transliterations in the section which includes chapters 6–36 made certain an Aramaic original for at least this portion of the book. Finally, in an article by the present writer, "Notes on the Greek Texts of Enoch," *Jour. Am. Or. Soc.*, 62 (1942), 52–60, it was shown that the entire book was composed in Aramaic.

Literature. See §9; also the article just mentioned.

§28. The Assumption of Moses

This little apocalypse, written in Palestine in the first years of the present era, has several features of interest. Aside from its significance as an early Jewish document, it has importance for the Christian Church inasmuch as verse 9 in the Epistle of Jude, concerning the strife of the archangel Michael with Satan over the body of Moses, is an allusion to the *Assumption*, as Origen, *De Principiis*, III, 2, 1, and others have testified. There is evidence that it was read with interest for many centuries.

The two versions of the work of which we have knowledge were made at an early date, first the Greek and from it the Latin. In the acts of the Second Nicene Council, of the year 787, there is mention of a book entitled Ἀνάληψις Μωυσέως, and its compass (stichometry) is given. At that time, then, the Greek text was still in circulation. We have no further news of the book, however, until late in the nineteenth century, when the famous Italian scholar Ceriani discovered in the Milan library a Latin palimpsest containing the first part of the work, about one third of the whole. Several lines are wanting at the beginning, and the text is otherwise defective and badly preserved. It is printed in Fritzsche's *Libri Apocryphi Vet. Test.*, pp. 700–729.

The part of the book that we possess is concerned mainly with Moses's prediction of the main events in the future history of Israel. Chapter 1 contains the instructions given by Moses to Joshua. Chapter 2 begins with the entrance into Canaan and continues to the end of the history of the Hebrew kingdoms. Chapter 3 treats of the Chaldeans, the destruction of Jerusalem, the deportation to a "country of the east," and captivity for "about seventy-seven years." Chapter 4 begins with Daniel and his prayer and carries the history through the time of Nehemiah. Chapter 5 then disposes of the early Greek period in general terms, but with evident allusion in verses 4 f. to the conditions described in 2 Macc. 4:7–20, and ends just before the rise of the Maccabees.

At this point the Latin text has met with an accident, the misplacement of a leaf. Chapters 8 and 9 (only a dozen verses in all) originally stood between chapters 5 and 6, as at once becomes obvious.

Chapter 8 (properly the sixth) begins with Antiochus Epiphanes, and is occupied solely with the horrors of his time. Chapter 9 (properly the seventh) introduces a man of the tribe of Levi who is given the mysterious name *Taxo* (see below). He addresses his "seven" sons, exhorting them to die rather than transgress the commands of the God of their fathers. Chapter 6 (properly the eighth) proceeds with a dynasty of kings and priests (the Hasmoneans); followed by "an insolent king," not a priest, whose reign of thirty-four years will be one of violence and bloodshed. His children also will bear rule, and in their time "a mighty king of the west" will come and inaugurate a reign of terror.

The vision has now reached the author's own day, and chapter 7 (properly the ninth) characterizes the evil time. Chapter 10 rehearses the signs and portents which will mark the end of the present age; and Joshua is exhorted to preserve faithfully all this revelation. Chapters 11 and 12 contain Joshua's words of grief and despair addressed to Moses, and the latter's comforting reply, which breaks off in the middle of a sentence (12:13). The account of the *assumption* of Moses which thereupon followed, and (as the stichometry shows, see above) oc-cupied the greater part of the book, is lost.

The date of the interesting little work is given approximately by the allusions in chapter 6. The "insolent king" whose reign lasted thirty-four years is Herod the Great (37–4 B.C.), as all interpreters have seen. In 6:7 it is confidently predicted that Herod's sons will have no such long reign as their father's. Such a prediction would hardly be made at any other time than near the beginning of these reigns;[101] moreover the next verse tells how these sons of Herod will be humbled by the king from the west, the reference being to the ruthless measures taken by Quintilius Varus in 4 B.C. Promise of unrest and change soon came in the case of Archelaus, who was deposed and banished after nine years of his reign. It was this, quite probably, that occa-sioned the guess in 6:7, and it may well be that the *Assumption* was written soon after this event (A.D. 6).

The original language of this apocalypse is determined by the solu-tion of the cryptic name "Taxo" in 9:1 (see above). In the *Jour. Bib. Lit.*, *62* (1943), 1–7, it was shown that the man intended is Matta-thias, the father of the Maccabees and of the Hasmonean dynasty. In the numerical value of the letters used "Taxo" corresponds exactly to "the Hasmonean," in Aramaic, but not in Hebrew. It was also con-jectured there that the "*seven* sons" (9:1) were made to represent the seven Hasmonean rulers, from Judas to Antigonus.

Literature. See §9.

§29. SECOND ESDRAS

THE title of the book exists in several different forms. The name "Second Esdras," adopted for the English versions, is taken from the first verse of the first chapter of the expanded book. In all the modern editions of the Latin Vulgate the title given is *Liber Esdrae Quartus*, whence the name "Fourth Ezra," commonly used on the continent of Europe. Another designation in frequent use is "The Apocalypse of Ezra." A more suitable title would be "The Apocalypse of Shealtiel," as will appear.

The Second Esdras which we have in our traditional collection is not the original work, but an expanded edition. Chapters 1, 2, 15, and 16 are wanting in all the oriental versions, and are generally recog-

---

101. As a matter of fact the guess was wrong; Philip and Herod Antipas reigned 37 and 43 years respectively.

nized as late additions made by Christian hands. Since they do not belong to O. T. literature, they are not given further mention here.[102] With the first verse of our *third* chapter the Jewish apocalypse begins.

The scene is the city of Babylon in the year 556 B.C., "the thirtieth year after the destruction of Jerusalem." Israel is in exile. The seer, in distress and trepidation, feeling his presumption but determined to plead the cause of his people, seeks to understand the dealing of the Most High with the children of Abraham. Why are the Gentiles prosperous while Israel is enslaved? Certainly no one of the nations of the earth is more righteous than Israel, in spite of the latter's disobedience.

An angel is sent to reply to the seer, and there follows a long debate. The revelation is given in a series of dream-visions, interrupted by periods of fasting or meditation. The author is concerned with the unsolved problems of human life and of unfolding history, the plan and the justice of God's dealing with mankind, from the creation to the end of the world. His discussion is one of the most important products of Jewish thought in the first years of the present era. Whether viewed as theology or as literature, it is a work of unusual originality and interest. By Christian readers it was held in high esteem from the first.

The seer begins with a sketch of Biblical history, in which he pays especial attention to Adam's fall, by reason of which all men inherited the "wicked heart" (3:21, 22, 26; 7:118). Coming to the present time, he compares captive Israel with the Babylonian oppressors, and seeks an explanation. The angel Uriel appears, and tells him that these matters are beyond human comprehension. His request for signs of the end is partially granted, and in chapter 5 a list of portents of the "last days" is given. He pleads again for his people: if the world was created for them, why may they not possess it? He is told that because of Adam's sin it is only through a narrow and toilsome passage, sorrowful and perilous (7:12), that entrance to the new and better world can be given. In chapters 7–9 [103] he is given instruction in several matters about which he has asked: the resurrection of the dead; the last judgment, when the books are opened; the Messianic period; the reason why the number of those who are to be saved is comparatively small.

102. In Fritzsche's *Libri Apocryphi Vet. Test.*, pp. 640–658, the Latin text of the four chapters is printed under the title "Liber Esdrae Quintus." In Wace's *Apocrypha,* J. H. Lupton includes the chapters in his commentary.

103. In the Apocrypha of the English A.V. chap. 7 is defective, with a gap of 70(!) verses between vss. 35 and 36. This gap was filled in 1875 upon the discovery of a Latin manuscript containing the complete text.

One of the visions is of a mourning woman whom the seer tries in vain to comfort. At the height of her distress she disappears in a flash, and in her place is the picture of a magnificent city. Thus are symbolized the past and the future of Zion.

Another symbolic picture of historical events is given in the famous Vision of the Eagle, in chapters 11 and 12, designed especially to show that the end of the present age is close at hand. In its original form the meaning of the vision was doubtless transparent, but there is evidence that it has received such additions and alterations as to make it perfectly incomprehensible.

In still another dream the seer is shown the advent of the warring and conquering Messiah, who takes his stand on a mountain and destroys the hostile armies by the flood of fire which issues from his mouth. Thereupon he calls the chosen people to his side, among them the lost ten tribes of Israel.

In the final (14th) chapter, Ezra the Scribe narrates how, at the command of God and under inspiration given for the purpose, he restored the Hebrew sacred literature which had been destroyed. This included not only the Law, the Prophets, and the canonical Writings, but also seventy "outside books." A draught from a divinely-given cup ensured perfect verbal recollection, and five amanuenses wrote from dictation, "in characters which they knew not," finishing the work in forty days. This took place, according to 14:48, five thousand years (plus a few added years, as well as certain months and days) after the creation of the world.[104]

The book thus treats of two quite distinct subjects, unrelated except in this, that both arise out of the supposed situation, Israel in captivity in Babylonia. The second subject is the origin of the written text of the Hebrew scriptures. The book of the Law, especially, cannot possibly have been with the exiles in Babylonia. If they had carried it with them, and then had given it no further notice, they certainly deserved to remain permanently in exile. Nor can the Law, the Prophets, and the other books have been left behind in Palestine; it was obvious that the Chaldeans had destroyed them. But when Ezra sets out for Jerusalem in the time of Artaxerxes he has the Law in his hand! Meditation on this miracle produced the story which here is told in detail.

The impression made by the fine work contained in chapters 1–13 is seriously marred by the fantastic tale in which Ezra appears. The tone of chapter 14 is noticeably different from that of the preceding

104. This date is wanting in the Latin version and its derivatives, including the English, probably because it was omitted when chapters 15 and 16 were added. The numbers of the years, months, and days appended to the 5,000 differ in the oriental versions. The date cannot be brought into relation with any known system of reckoning from the creation, and its purpose may be merely mystification (see below).

chapters, and it is plain that an incongruous element has been appended to the original apocalypse. A premonition of this was given at the very beginning of the book, where we read: "In the thirtieth year after the ruin of the city, I Shealtiel [105] (*the same is Ezra*) was in Babylon, and lay troubled upon my bed," etc. The prince Shealtiel, the son of Jehoiachin, who at the time supposed was in virtual charge of captive Israel (as Paltiel the captain of their guard reminds him in 5:17), was by no one supposed to be identical with Ezra the priest and scribe who lived many years later. G. H. Box, in Charles's *Apocrypha*, II, 549, gives what he correctly terms the only adequate explanation. The seer who was the recipient of the revelations spoke in the name of Shealtiel. "The compiler who utilized this written source was anxious, for some reason, to connect it with the name of Ezra; accordingly he inserted the words *who am also Ezra*."

It is obvious that with the same purpose the name of Ezra was interpolated in 6:10, 7:2, 25; 8:2.[106] Addressing the seer by name is somewhat unusual and therefore the more noticeable. Possibly the interpolator inserted also the clause in 10:57b, to call attention to the preceding examples of such address. On the other hand, the superscription in 8:19b, with its mention of Ezra, is known to be a late addition to the Latin text, brought about by the fact that the eloquent prayer which follows was often copied separately and furnished with a title.

The transition from the apocalypse of Shealtiel to the narrative of Ezra and the Scriptures is made easy and natural by a few verses inserted near the end of chapter 13. The portion of the text which is secondary is readily recognized when the fact of the transition is seen. It includes verses 53b–56 and the last sentence of verse 58: "And there I sat three days." Thus the passage is explained by G. H. Box (see above), and the present writer had independently made exactly the same analysis. The Shealtiel-apocalypse appears to have its original ending in 13:57, 58, with the omission above mentioned.

An approximate date of the apocalypse was originally provided by *the eagle vision* in chapters 11 and 12, but there is good evidence that the details of the vision have been so changed and multiplied that their meaning is now obscure.

One Jewish apocalyptist after another attempted to give definite information, through the medium of some mysterious imagery, as to the end of the present age; the outstanding examples are the books of Daniel and Revelation. Each saw how the history of the world as it

---

105. Since it now is well established that the original language of the apocalypse was Semitic, the Hebrew forms of the proper names are to be preferred.

106. Box recognizes these as insertions, it is to be noted.

concerned his people had reached a climax which could only mean that the great day was at hand. He was assured of this, otherwise he would not have written his book with its announcement given in the form of a divine revelation. As one prediction after another proved to be mistaken, the successive documents could be put aside, or reinterpreted, or even revised. The work now before us seems to be an important example of such revision, the symbolism which gave the mistaken date being altered in such a way as to give a less distinct indication *of a later date*.

The numerous wings of the eagle represent successive Roman emperors, and it is plain that the first century A.D. is already far advanced. The picture of the eagle, however, has been made an indescribable chaos, seemingly with deliberate intent. Along with the wings are now heads, variously interpreted. Scholars in increasing number have become convinced that new and disturbing features have been introduced into the vision. The basal number of the wings (emperors), originally *eight* (11:11), is increased to *twelve*, evidently for the sake of a later dating.

The three heads that were "preserved for the last" (11:9), restoring the empire to its first estate when it had seemed in peril of falling (12:18), permitted by the Most High to "renew many things" (12:23), are unquestionably the emperors Vespasian, Titus, and Domitian, as is generally agreed. With these three the number of emperors is increased to eleven, and the probability appears that the later editor attached to the sacred number *twelve* the same significance that the author of Revelation gave to the number *seven* (Rev. 17:9–11). Writing in the time of Domitian, he was confident that in the days of *the next* emperor the doom of wicked Rome would be sealed. Nevertheless, he so expanded the picture of the eagle with the appearance of twenty or twenty-three wings (11:11; 12:19) that the history of the empire could, if necessary, be carried on farther—as in some modern commentaries.

The portion of the symbolism which provided the all-important date, the date of the Shealtiel Apocalypse, appears to be still recognizable; but it behooves the interpreter to present any theory with the utmost diffidence.

The lion roaring from the wood (11:37; 12:31 f.) is the Messiah, (namely, the son of Ephraim, see 7:28 f.; the insertion here is wrong), who announces the end of the present age; his advent marked the climax of the original vision. It is important to ascertain, if possible, what preceding events in Roman history had seemed to show that the end was at hand. First, however, it is to be noticed that the author does not confine himself to the imperial history, but in 12:2, 30 takes notice of a small, "feeble kingdom" (*regnum exile*), "full of trouble" (*turbatio*). In this there were two rulers who felt themselves to be in the royal class (12:2). This can hardly be anything else than the Judean kingdom, the two rulers intended being the two outstanding kings of Herod's family, Agrippa I and Agrippa II, the former still held in vivid memory, the latter present in person. Their "feeble kingdom" was to remain up to the very end (12:30), *the Most High had preserved it.*

As to the latest of the Roman emperors known to the author of the Shealtiel Apocalypse: the three who are the last before the advent of the lion are given some description which may give help. Last of all come two "heads" (originally "wings"?), who are rivals (11:34 f., 12:21 end, 27 f.). Immediately preceding them was a great emperor who "held the whole earth in possession, and bare rule . . . with much oppression, and had the governance of the world more than all the wings that had been" (11:32). There is one emperor, and only one, to whom this could apply, namely, Nero. No other had made so deep a personal impression, not only in Rome but throughout the whole Roman world. The cruelty and oppression of his later years, and especially the dreadful scenes in Rome in the year 64, had aroused horror in the east, as we know especially from the book of Revelation.[107]

In 12:26 there is allusion to the manner of the "great" emperor's death: he "shall die upon his bed, and yet with pain." This plainly refers to Nero's suicide, with a short sword, "on his bed." Thereupon follows brief mention of the end, after violent rivalry, of Nero's two immediate successors, Galba and Otho. The sword of Otho slew Galba (11:35; 12:28); the death of the former by the sword is also predicted (a perfectly safe prediction, and soon fulfilled), but it seems plain from the last words of 12:28, compare 11:35 f., that the apocalyptist had not yet heard of the death of Otho, which took place on the 16th of April of the year 69, but cannot have been known in the east until some time later.

The conclusion seems justified, therefore, that the Apocalypse of Shealtiel was published in the first months of the year named. This tallies with the fact that the work shows no knowledge of the catastrophe of the year 70. The accusation of the Fourth Beast in 11:40–42, covering its entire history, could hardly have been couched in such general terms, throughout, after the armies of Titus had laid waste the holy city and burned the temple.

107. It is characteristic of the obscuring alteration of the vision, at a later day, that the wide rule and oppression of this emperor is distributed among *three* "heads"(!) in 12:24, in the interpretation. Notice also the abrupt change at 12:26 (cf. 11:33, which has also been retouched).

Further confirmation is given by the symbolism of the eight wings (11:11), unquestionably the original number but increased later, as was remarked above. The eight emperors are Julius, Augustus (particularly mentioned in 12:15), Tiberius, Caligula, Claudius, Nero, Galba, and Otho.[108]

Comparison of this Apocalypse with the N. T. Revelation is most instructive. The latter was written in the year 68, in the reign of Galba (*Documents of the Primitive Church*, pp. 225–244). It is evident that when chaos followed the tragic death of Nero after the horror of his reign, the learned men of Palestine, whether Jews or Christians, were so sure of the approaching End that they could make definite predictions. Those made in Revelation were obscure enough to be allowed to stand; but as Vespasian, Titus, and Domitian came upon the scene, the five visions of Shealtiel were discredited as prophecy, for the "eight wings" and the plain allusions to Nero, Galba, and Otho spoke loudly of a mistaken guess! Hence the new edition of the eagle imagery (shown with especial clearness by the alteration of 11:32 in 12:23 f.!). One feature of it is the three heads, another the twelve wings, and along with these a number of details designed for mystification; leaving however the semblance of a prediction that the End would come in the time of the twelfth emperor, the successor of Domitian.

There is strong evidence that this rehabilitation of the book was directly connected with the appending of the Ezra vision which now constitutes chapter 14. It seems probable that *all* of the Ezra material contained in "Second Esdras" came into being at one and the same time, namely, in and for the revision which gave to the neglected but noble work a new name and a new life. This was at some time in the reign of Domitian (81–96). It is possible that the curious date in 14:48 (see above) was added with the purpose of making the existing obscurity still more obscure.

The question of the original language of the Shealtiel-Apocalypse is not easily settled, for the Greek translation is lost, and we must rely on secondary versions, especially the Syriac and the Latin, which were made from the Greek. In recent years it has become increasingly clear that the original language of the book was Semitic; and in the *Jour. Bib. Lit.*, *61* (1942), 72–74, good reason was given for deciding in favor of Aramaic rather than Hebrew. This would presumably include the Ezra vision (chap. 14), but no definite evidence there has appeared.

For a clear understanding of the history of this book and of its

108. Otho's accession was recognized in the east more generally than in the west, as Tacitus, *Hist.*, I, 76, informs us. Vitellius was not thus recognized.

transformation a study of its rival, the Apocalypse of Baruch, is necessary. See accordingly the next following section.

Literature. See §9; also B. Violet, *Die Esra-Apokalypse* (1910), containing, in translation, the text of all the ancient versions. L. Gry, *Les dires prophétiques d'Esdras,* 2 vols. (1937), arguing for an Aramaic original. Schürer has a full account of the discussion regarding the book.

§30. THE APOCALYPSE OF BARUCH

THIS is commonly entitled "The Syriac Apocalypse of Baruch," for it is completely preserved only in the Syriac version, which is a rendering from the Greek, no longer extant, which was translated from the original Aramaic. Among the other works attributed to Baruch there is at least one apocalypse.

The seer received the divine revelation in a series of visions, beginning "in the 25th year of Jehoiachin king of Judah" (1:1). This somewhat surprising date would correspond to the year 590 B.C., see 2 Kings 24:8. From 6:1 we learn that it was on the day before the Chaldean armies arrived and surrounded the city; that is, in the tenth month of the year 587, see 2 Kings 25:1. The deportation of Zedekiah is mentioned in 8:5. It would be fruitless, and is unnecessary, to attempt to harmonize the two dates.

It is important at the outset to consider the close relation existing between this Apocalypse and the Apocalypse of Shealtiel ("Second Esdras"). The fact of a literary connection has long been noticed, and at present it is generally agreed that the author of the one work made direct use of the other, and this not in a few places but throughout the whole composition. R. H. Charles, *The Apocalypse of Baruch* (1896), pp. 170 f., lists between sixty and seventy passages in Baruch which have their counterpart in Shealtiel.

It is possible to characterize the relation more definitely, as purposeful imitation. The imitator was impressed with the authority of his predecessor, and would rival and surpass it. A few typical examples of the duplication may be given. An important feature of each apocalypse, determining the character of the whole work, is the debate at the beginning. The seer questions the Most High concerning the plan for his chosen people; why is Israel trampled upon, while the Babylonian oppressors are prosperous? The argument of the one seer duplicates that of the other, and numerous passages are verbally parallel.

In both works an unusual amount of attention is paid to Adam's fall and its consequences. More than this, each author utters the cry: "O Adam, what hast thou done to all those that are born from thee?" S 7:118=B 48:42. The one borrows verbally from the other.

In each of the two apocalypses the visions are interrupted by fasts of seven days. On the occasion of one of the fasts the seer prepares to go into retirement, and the people cry, "Why do you leave us? If you forsake us, it were better that we should all die." He answers, "I have not forsaken you; I am going to pray for Zion, and will return to you." B 32:7–9=S 12:40–49. The wording of the one long passage is slavishly copied from the other. Many similar examples could be given.

Since the one apocalypse is designed to improve upon the other, which it openly duplicates, it is obvious that the work which claims the earlier date and the greater name is the borrower, for it thus eclipses its rival and holds the field. Few would believe, in the present case, that the man who copied out the words and visions of Baruch the son of Neriah, the companion and helper of Jeremiah, could then consign his own book to oblivion by dating it a quarter of a century later and ascribing it to a man so nearly unknown as Shealtiel.

The Apocalypse of Baruch does in fact look like an enlarged and (in intention) improved edition of the "Second Esdras" apocalypse. In general, the teaching of B is the same as that of S, while normally more expanded and detailed; thus for example in the doctrine of the resurrection (chaps. 49–51), and in the pictures of the Messianic age (chaps. 29 f., 39 f., where the crude chiliasm of the former passage is especially noteworthy). Both apocalypses are thoroughly Jewish and characteristic of their time. At one point there is a note of disagreement, as all the commentators have observed. S holds a pessimistic view of the power of the "evil heart" inherited from Adam, and gives his conviction frequent expression. Against this, B would emphasize the freedom of the will: "Though Adam first sinned and brought untimely death upon us all, yet . . . each one of us has been the Adam of his own soul" (54:15, 19).

The literary style of B is inferior, and its paragraphs are often loosely constructed, the thought of the writer leaving the main theme temporarily for some subordinate subject. There is no lack of originality, however, and the book contains very much that is of interest. There is a thorough study of its theology and of its literary relations by Louis Ginzberg in the *Jewish Encyclopedia*.

Two of the visions may be given special mention. The parable of the forest, the vine, the fountain, and the cedar (chaps. 35 ff.) brings the history of Israel down to the writer's own time. The cedar, the last tree left standing in the forest, represents the Roman empire. The time of its destruction comes, and it is to be burned. The vine (Israel) pronounces its doom and recounts its crimes, charging it with wickedness, harshness, and arrogance (but with no implication of any evil done to the vine itself). The opening words uttered by the vine: "Art thou not that cedar?" etc., and the details of the following accusation, are shamelessly imitated from the parallel in S, 11:39 ff., which begins: "Art thou not that fourth beast?" etc.

The other vision is the parable of the thunder-cloud pouring out waters clear or inky in turn (chaps. 53, 56–70). Israelite history is made to fall into twelve periods,[109] alternately good and evil, symbolized by the color of the water from the cloud. The first period was black, from Adam's sin to the deluge; then followed a bright period, including Abraham and the patriarchs; and so on. The inky waters of the eleventh period (chap. 67) symbolized the Babylonian captivity. The twelfth period, with its clear waters, represented the Restoration and the subsequent history of Israel among the nations. At the end, after the alternations of good and evil, there is pictured a period unlike the others. It concerns not Israel chiefly, but "belongs to the whole world" (69:1). The cloud still pours, but the water is now black and mingled with fire, and lightning deals destruction. This is the time of confusion and uproar in which the Messiah strikes down his enemies, the picture corresponding to that which is given in S's chapter 13. The lightning in B corresponds to the devastating fire from the Messiah's mouth in the former picture; the rescued people seeking the protection of the lightning (53:11) are those who assembled to the divine warrior in S 13:12 f.

The apocalyptist continues awkwardly in chapter 72, marring his figure of the waters by returning and adding to it after it had been finished and laid aside (71:2). The angel proceeds: "Hear now also concerning the clear waters that are to come at the end, after the black waters. This is what will take place." He first describes briefly the judgment to be visited upon the nations and the separation of the good among them from the evil, this in 72:2–6; then in the two chapters 73 and 74 he paints an inspiring picture of the coming era of peace, gladness, good will, and fruitful labor. "These," he says at the end (74:4), "are the last clear waters which followed the last black waters" (followed them, that is, in 72:1, nowhere else).[110]

109. This division seems to be taken over and significantly improved by the author of *the Ezra-appendage to S* (2 Esd. 14:11).

110. Charles (*Apocalypse of Baruch*, pp. 114, 116; *Apocrypha*, II, 518), who supposed that the angel is still interpreting details of Baruch's vision, would emend "the bright waters" of 72:1 to "the bright lightning"; and similarly "these are the last bright waters," in 74:4, to "this is the bright lightning." The suggestion has been adopted,

It seems quite evident from 68:5–7 followed by 70:2–6 (compare also chap. 27) that the author wrote before the catastrophe of the year 70. Against this conclusion stands the verse 32:3, with its direct allusion to the destruction of Jerusalem and the temple by the Romans. The context of the passage is to be noted. "The time is coming," Baruch says in 32:1, "when the Almighty *will shake the whole creation.*" This inevitably recalls Hag. 2:6 and the prophet's continuation: "The latter glory of this house shall be greater than the former." Some reader of B felt that the prophet Baruch should here show his knowledge of the *second* destruction of Jerusalem and therefore inserted verses 2–4, paraphrasing Haggai and in verse 3 predicting the great disaster. Charles, in both of his editions, brackets verses 2–4, with good reason; but whether the *whole* passage is secondary or not, who will believe that the Jewish author and patriot who had seen the devastation wrought by the armies of Titus could have been satisfied to make this one colorless allusion in his great picture of Jewish history?

Any conjecture is precarious, but what the evidence appears to show is that B was written immediately after S, and that it did in fact eclipse its rival. The latter was then buried from sight until the reign of Domitian, when it was resurrected and restored to high favor by being made over into an Ezra-Apocalypse in the manner described in the preceding chapter.

B makes the impression of a continuous composition, homogeneous throughout. No good reason has appeared for questioning its unity. The problem of the original language is the same which was encountered in S. It is now quite generally agreed that the book is a Semitic composition, and Hebrew has been taken for granted. There is clear evidence, however, that both apocalypses were written in Aramaic, see the article referred to in the former case.

Literature. See §9.

§31. JUBILEES

THE book of Jubilees is in form a midrashic targum on Genesis and Exodus. It is much more than this, however, for it is a treatise with an apologetic purpose thoroughly accomplished. It aims to show that the Judaism of its day had existed as normative from the very beginning

e.g., by Ryssel in Kautzsch's *Apokryphen.* But the lightning, like the torrent of fire in S, symbolizes only *the warring* Messiah, it could not represent his peaceful reign, the circumstances pictured in chaps. 73 and 74. The text is right as it stands, in both places.

of human history. It would also demonstrate that the sacred number *seven* played a more important part in history than had generally been understood.

The book describes itself at the outset (in 1:1) as the history of the *division* (partition, distribution) of "the days of the law and the testimony, of the events of the years, of their year-weeks, and of their jubilees, throughout all the years of the world." The whole history of the world is divided into "jubilee" periods, cycles of 7 x 7 years (see Lev. 25:8–12), and the subdivisions of this chronological system are in sevens.

The plan of the work is that of a revelation given to Moses on Mount Sinai on the occasion described in Ex. 24:12–18. The "Angel of the Presence" recounts to him in detail all the history that is of interest to the Hebrews from the creation of the world to the passage through the Red Sea, and reveals to him an oral law in addition to the written law. The latter was to be made known to all, but the former was to be kept as a tradition privately transmitted. This oral law is by no means represented as new in any part; it had been known to the patriarchs and faithfully observed by them. Moses is commanded to write all this down.

From 2:1 onward, accordingly, the book runs parallel to the Biblical history from Gen. 1:1 to Ex. 14:31, with constant midrashic expansion and in an atmosphere very different from that of the original narrative. There is never-failing emphasis on the characteristically Jewish tenets and customs and on the right observance of the several feasts. The contrast between Jews and Gentiles is sharply drawn, and Israel is to be kept strictly separate. The development of angelology and demonology has progressed farther than in Enoch. We now meet with Beliar (1:20; 15:33) and Mastēmā (10:8 and frequently), sure signs of a late date.[111] Charles, *Apocrypha*, II, 10, shows how closely the doctrine of angels and demons resembles that in the New Testament. There is also in Jubilees a large amount of legendary matter that had gradually taken shape in Jewish folklore. A characteristic feature of the book is the omission of such details in the history of the patriarchs as could show any one of them in an unfavorable light.

From the passage 4:17–21 especially it is certain that the author of

111. Beliar is derived from the "Belial" of the Hebrew scriptures, the phonetic variation having merely the purpose of gaining a proper name. Mastēm, "enemy," in form an Aramaic participle, is another artificial name. The root (also Hebrew) is a variation of the one from which the name "Satan" is derived. The final -ā is the Aramaic definite ending. It was probably from this name that the (late) Hebrew *mastema,* "enmity," was coined. It appears in Hos. 9:7, 8, in both cases later than the LXX version and not represented in either Syriac or Targum. It is found also in the *Documents of a Zadokite Sect* (see below).

the work was well acquainted with the book of Enoch. On the other hand, Jubilees appears to have been used in the Testaments of the Twelfth Patriarchs, a work which is perhaps best dated at about the end of the last century B.C. or in the beginning of the 1st century A.D. (see the section dealing with it). The fact that the author of Jubilees (who is generally recognized as a Levite priest) takes pride in the institution of the Hasmonean priesthood by no means puts him in the time of John Hyrcanus, as some have argued. That pride is even more noticeable in the Testament of Levi (8:15), and it might have been felt as long as any enthusiasm for the Hasmonean house remained alive.

The evidence of date given by the presence of the names Beliar and Mastēmā was mentioned above. Judging from the known occurrences of these names, they belong to a late period in the history of the "outside books." Beliar is found in the Sibylline Oracles, III, 69 ff., and in the Ascension of Isaiah, these both generally recognized as of the 1st century A.D.; in the Testaments (in nearly every one of the twelve!), of approximately the same date, as will appear; also, several times, in the Lives of the Prophets, a work originally Hebrew, perhaps of the 1st century and certainly not earlier.

Mastēm appears twelve times in Jubilees, always with the Aramaic definite ending, Mastema, "*the* Enemy." It seems to be present also in Judith 4:6 and 14:4 (see the section on Judith) in the pseudonym of Samaria, Βετομασθεμ, "House of Satan," the θ in the Greek transcription corresponding to the manner of writing the name in the Ethiopic version. From the name, apparently, was derived the late Hebrew abstract noun *mastema*, "enmity," which is found in the *Documents of a Zadokite Sect*, 20:5, immediately following a verse which mentions the book of Jubilees. The Zadokite work, which contains a reference to the Testament of Levi, cannot be earlier than the first century A.D. At about this time, as the existing evidence seems to show, the Hebrew noun must have been introduced into the text of Hos. 9:7, 8.

The second half of the last century B.C. may be conjectured as the period within whose limits the composition of Jubilees is to be placed. There appears no good ground for a more definite dating.

Aside from the title "Jubilees," which was the one in ordinary use, the book was given some other names in early literature. The most common of these was "the Little Genesis," the adjective apparently designed to contrast this secondary and uncanonical account with the far greater book of Moses. In the Ethiopic version the title is simply "Book of the Division."

The history of the transmission of the text is almost exactly like that which has been described in the case of Enoch. The original language was Aramaic, not Hebrew as has generally been supposed. (Littmann, in Kautzsch, *Apokryphen*, II, 34, was inclined to decide for Aramaic, but allowed himself to be persuaded.) "Mastemā" gives striking evidence, as has been shown, and there are numerous other indications. Charles himself has remarked (*Book of Jubilees*, p. 100) that in Gen. 14:14 it is not the Hebrew but the Targum that is followed. See also *Jour. Bib. Lit., 61* (1942), 72. We should hardly expect a revision *in Hebrew* of the solely authoritative text of Genesis and Exodus. Targums are another matter.

The original text disappeared at a very early date. The Greek translation, which seems to have been carefully made, is also lost, with the exception of a few quotations. The book is completely preserved only in the Ethiopic version, apparently a faithful rendering of the Greek. A Latin version, also made from the Greek, is extant for only a minor portion of the book. It is contained in Charles's excellent edition of the Ethiopic text.

Literature. See §9; also R. H. Charles, *The Book of Jubilees* (1902), Introduction, translation, and notes. H. Rönsch, *Das Buch der Jubiläen* (1874).

§32. The Testaments of the Twelve Patriarchs

This book belongs to a class of literature that seems to have been especially popular at about the beginning of the present era and for a time thereafter. Old legends of patriarchs and prophets were collected and new ones were composed. The titles of many such works are given in the Christian Church lists of canonical and apocryphal books (see the General Introduction), and it appears that the bulk of this literature perished at an early date. The surviving specimens, more or less fragmentary, include legends of Moses, the books of Adam and Eve, the Ascension of Isaiah, an Apocalypse of Abraham (Schürer, *Geschichte*, III, 250), and the Lives of the Prophets. One of the lost books, that of Jannes and Jambres, is referred to in the New Testament, 2 Tim. 3:8, as has already been mentioned.

This miniature of the twelve tribes of Israel, the "Testaments," has its own distinct character and is a work of some importance. The general pattern was given by Genesis 49, where Jacob, about to die, gathers his sons at his bedside and foretells their future; also by Deuteronomy 33, where Moses blesses the twelve, one by one, as tribes destined to triumph, each in its own way. In the Testaments, on the contrary, prediction plays only a minor part.

Each of the sons of Jacob, as he sees his end approaching, calls his own sons about him to receive his last instructions. *First*, he rehearses for their benefit the most significant events of his life, emphasizing either the sin with which his name had been associated, or else the virtue which his life had exemplified. The picture in each case is not obtained solely from the Biblical narratives, but numerous legendary details are also added. *Next*, he draws for his hearers a practical lesson from what he has just told them; they must take warning and avoid the sin which he had committed (this applied to the most of the patriarchs), or they must emulate the virtues of which they had heard. The ethical instruction which is thus given is the most noticeable feature of the Testaments. It struck a new note, characteristic of its day, and was a chief reason for the amount of attention which the book received. *Finally*, the patriarch enters the apocalyptic field, telling his sons what will take place in the last days. This feature occupies very little space, however, and in the case of one tribe, Gad, is omitted altogether.

Reuben warns his sons against unchastity and its evils, referring to his own sin described in Gen. 35:22 and 49:4. Simeon tells of the harm wrought by envy and bitter rivalry; it was in punishment for his malice against Joseph that he was held as a hostage in Egypt (Gen. 42:24). Levi in 6:7 confesses to undue violence in the case of Shechem (Gen. 34), but in the main is glorified both in the past history and in the prediction of the future. He seems in fact to stand at the head of the Twelve. Judah warns his sons against wine, women, and greed, narrating such episodes in his early life as only late haggada could invent; and he foretells the coming of the Messianic ruler from his tribe. Issachar boasts of his prosperity as a brawny and virtuous laborer in field and farm (Gen. 49:14 f.). Zebulun charges his sons to show such pity and compassion as he himself had shown throughout his life. He was a famous fisherman, claiming also the honor of being the first to devise mast and sail for his boat (5:5–6:3). Dan warned against enmity and falsehood, referring to his treatment of his brother Joseph (conduct not recorded elsewhere). Naphtali called for harmony; let everything be done in order and in its proper season. Gad, who had shown his hatred of Joseph (not mentioned in any other place), urges his children to love their brothers and kinsmen. Asher commands: Be not double-faced, but follow the truth in singleness of heart. Joseph describes at length and in much detail his temptation in Egypt, and charges his sons to be steadfast in chastity. Benjamin's testament is the exhortation to "be like Joseph"; keep a pure mind, flee from malice, live a blameless life.

Some evidence of the popularity which the book enjoyed may be seen in the history of its transmission. It is preserved entire in Greek, and there are two types of the text, the one presumably derived from the other by memory, as usual. The Armenian version, made from the Greek, has proved to be important, especially for demonstrating the Christian interpolations in the text. It is a remarkable fact that no trace of a Latin version has been found. A late Hebrew Testament of Naphtali is extant, and there are considerable Aramaic fragments of the Testament of Levi in the libraries at Oxford and Cambridge; these all translated in Charles, *Apocrypha*, II, 361–367. The original language of the book was Hebrew, as is abundantly evident from the Greek. The mistranslation in Levi 6:10 (see Charles's note) would be sufficient proof, even if there were no other.

Further evidence of the popularity of the Testaments appears in the amount of interpolation and expansion that the text has received, especially from Christian hands. There was a time when the prevailing critical estimate of the whole work made it a Christian composition, but more careful study and the testimony of the Armenian version showed that the Christian material is secondary. It is quite unmistakable in many places, especially in the Testament of Benjamin, chapters 3, 9–11, the last-named containing a plain allusion to the apostle Paul.

The date of the work is determined approximately by the facts already set forth. We have seen that the book is later than Jubilees, which is assigned to the latter part of the last century B.C. The emphasis on ethical teaching (see above), the relatively slight attention paid to legal observances, even in the Testament of Levi, and the advanced stage of development reached in the haggada, all point to a late date. While the last years of the closing century B.C. cannot be ruled out, the first years of the present era seem the more probable time for the composition of the book.

Literature. See §9.

§33. THE BOOK OF ADAM AND EVE

THIS book is known in several forms, usually under the title "Life of Adam and Eve," as in the Latin version. The Greek text, published from several manuscripts in 1866, was given by its editor the unsuitable title "Apocalypse of Moses," and it is commonly referred to under this name. Other versions which have been translated and made accessible are the Armenian and the Slavonic. It is to be presumed that all these types of text go back to a single Greek translation made from the Jewish (and Semitic) archetype. Their rather wide variation is

doubtless largely due to the reproduction from memory which would
be normal in such folklore as this. There are many insertions and additions made by Christian hands, generally to be recognized without
difficulty. The book is mainly pure haggada; incidents in the life of
Adam and Eve not furnished by the Biblical narrative are here
supplied.

To Adam were assigned the northern and eastern parts of the garden, to Eve the southern and western parts. In the hour when their
two guardian angels had gone up to worship, the devil saw and used
his opportunity. As Eve tastes the fruit of the forbidden tree, the
immediate result is knowledge of her nakedness. She looks for leaves
to make a girdle, but the trees refuse and their leaves all disappear,
with the single exception of the fig tree.

When Adam is expelled from the garden, he is permitted to take
with him certain spices and a variety of seeds for planting. At first,
however, he and his wife finding themselves unable to eat grass (4:1 f.)
must go hungry for many days. Adam decides that they must do penance: he will stand on a stone in the river Jordan, with the water up
to his neck, for forty days; Eve must do the same in the Tigris for
thirty-seven days. Adam does his full time; but Eve, chilled and shak-
ing like grass in the wind (10:1), is enticed out of the river by Satan,
who lies to her.

The circumstances of the birth of Cain are described at some
length. As soon as the babe is born he runs and plucks a blade of grass
and brings it to his mother. The murder of Abel and the birth of Seth
are very briefly narrated. Adam describes to Seth the flight from
Paradise. Eden was surrounded by great rivers, but Michael touched
the water with his rod and it froze, so the fugitives went across on the
ice. Then follows, in 29:4–10, the account of a vision which Adam saw
as a result of his eating of the tree of knowledge, a look into the distant
future. What he saw in regard to the successive temples at Jerusalem
may be of help in dating the book (see below).

In Adam's last days he suffers acute pain. Seth in distress asks:
"What is pain, my lord father?" He was soon to learn. Eve and her
son set out for the region of Paradise in the hope of getting a drop of
oil of the tree of mercy (36:2), to cure Adam. On the way they are
attacked by a wild beast (for the animal nature, like the human, had
fallen from grace), and Seth is bitten. At the gates of Paradise they
are told that the oil can be had only at the end of the present age, and
that Adam will die in six days.

In the Greek version ("Apocalypse of Moses," 15:1–29:7) Eve now
assembles her children and grandchildren and gives them a detailed
account of her transgression and of its immediate consequences, dwell-

ing especially on the scene in Eden when judgment was pronounced. Michael blows his trumpet and assembles the host of heaven. As God enters Paradise on his chariot of cherubim, with the angels singing in chorus, all the trees in every part of the garden shoot forth blossoms. There follows an extended paraphrase of Gen. 3:9–19. The book ends with the death and burial of the two.

A date in the 1st century A.D. is indicated for these legends. The haggada closely resembles that which has so important a part in Jubilees and the Testaments of the Twelve Patriarchs. The little apocalypse in 29:4–10, which evidently is brought down to the time of the author himself, shows no knowledge of the destruction of Jerusalem and the temple in the year 70. Verse 6 tells of the return of the exiles from Babylonia, and of the building of the second temple; and continues: "and in the last time the house of God will be exalted greater than of old." L. S. A. Wells, in Charles's *Apocrypha*, II, 140, would refer this to the temple of the Messianic age; but the text proceeds: "And once more iniquity will exceed righteousness." This seems to make necessary the reference to Herod's temple, as several commentators have concluded.

Study of the Greek text, namely, of the "Apocalypse of Moses" in Tischendorf's *Apocalypses Apocryphae* (1866), leaves no doubt that the original language of the work was Aramaic. The evidence of this is pervasive and unmistakable.

Literature. See §9; also M. R. James, *The Lost Apocrypha of the Old Testament* (1920).

§34. The "Martyrdom of Isaiah"

The case of this "book" is peculiar, for the bit of narrative commonly treated as a Jewish work, *The Martyrdom of Isaiah,* is such only by very doubtful conjecture. It is not clear that it, or any considerable part of it in its present verbal form, ever stood in a Jewish document.

It is beyond doubt that in the Palestinian tradition the prophet Isaiah suffered martyrdom in the manner described here; the story is told in the Lives of the Prophets, which is a collection of originally Jewish legends and traditions, hardly later than the 1st century, and it is very probably alluded to in the New Testament, Heb. 11:37, in the words "they were sawn asunder."

There is in early literature no mention of any writing entitled "The Martyrdom of Isaiah." The belief of modern scholars that such a document had existed is obtained from certain passages in the works of Origen; see the references in Schürer, III, 283. These passages will be discussed presently. There is mention of a Vision of Isaiah in the "List of the Sixty Canonical Books" (see the General Introduction, §6), and an Ascension of Isaiah is mentioned by Epiphanius and Jerome. The latter work was unknown until 1819, when a complete Ethiopic version was discovered and published by Richard Laurence, with translations in Latin and English. It is only from this work that our text of the supposed Martyrdom is obtained. The Vision had been known in a Latin translation since 1522, and it was now found to consist of chapters 6–11 of the Ascension, which is unquestionably a Christian work throughout. Chapters 1–5 of the latter, comprising perhaps the amount of three octavo pages, are mainly narrative, but contain also Isaiah's prediction of Jesus and the Christian Church (3:13–4:18). The narrative, loosely constructed, deals at first with Hezekiah, his son Manasseh, Isaiah, and the Hebrew prophets of that time, and in chapter 5 tells the story of Isaiah's martyrdom. It is in these introductory chapters of the Ascension that search has been made for a Jewish apocryphon.

Now Origen nowhere claims to have seen a *Jewish* work dealing with the prophet's martyrdom. He is sure that the tradition came originally from the Jews, and in saying this he more than once refers to the passage in the Epistle to the Hebrews, above mentioned. That Epistle, clearly, is the authority for his belief that the tradition is Jewish. He himself had seen the story "in a certain apocryphal Isaiah." What apocryphon this was, is apparent from his Homily on Isaiah, I, 5 (Schürer, *ibid.*), where he quotes verbally from our Ascension, 3:8–10! Origen, then, gives no testimony whatever to the existence of a separate writing containing the story of the martyrdom.

It was a reasonable conjecture, though lacking any support in the document itself,[112] that the original of our Ethiopic work was composite, and that the first chapters (just which?) were taken from a Jewish source. But the conjecture fails to find any support. Several attempts at analysis have been made, but have gained no general agreement. Especially from Charles's discussion, *Apocrypha*, II, 157, it seems quite evident that the attempt to sift out the fragments of a Jewish document must be fruitless.

The Ethiopic version of the Ascension is an able rendering from the

112. More than one commentator remarks that chapter 6 begins "an entirely new section." Naturally so. The prophet is dead, and this is the time to tell of the vision which he had seen, and of his ascension to heaven. The author of the book could not well avoid beginning a "totally new chapter" at 6:1! There is no change in the character of the language.

Greek, as is generally agreed. The question of a Semitic text behind the Greek in some part of the first five chapters can hardly arise, for there is next to nothing on which to base an answer to it. The material used here by the author of the book no doubt came *ultimately* from Jewish legends, but more than this can hardly be said with any confidence. The name of the "man of Samaria" (2:12), who betrayed the prophet to Manasseh and rejoiced in his death, is a good Aramaic (not Hebrew) personal name, *Bechīrā*, "the chosen, approved." [113] There is this very slight ground for conjecturing that the legend from which the Christian author derived his account was Aramaic.

We have thus no particle of evidence of a separate document, Jewish or Christian, that could be entitled "The Martyrdom of Isaiah."

Literature. See §9.

§35. The Lives of the Prophets

THIS once-popular work, for a long time nearly lost to sight and in modern times rarely mentioned, deserves to be included in the list of the "outside books." It exists in a number of Greek forms, and there are also Syriac, Latin, and Ethiopic versions. It is a catalogue of the Hebrew prophets designed especially to tell the origin of each of their number, where he was born, to what tribe or people he belonged, and in what place he was buried. Whatever other biographical details are included are those which were current in the Jewish popular legends. The Biblical material is not repeated, but is supplemented.

The Palestinian origin of the document is obvious, and so also is the early date. The framework of these lives has distinctly the sound of the Old Testament, and there are details of Palestinian geography which are not found in the Bible. The original language of the work was Hebrew (see below), and all the existing texts are derived from a single Greek translation. The Hebrew original was destroyed, along with the other extra-canonical writings in Hebrew or Aramaic, at about the end of the first century of the present era; see the General Introduction, §3.

The form of the Greek text which has been best known is that which is found in editions of the writings of Epiphanius, Bishop of Salamis in Cyprus (*c.* 315–403). It is not, however, in any part his own

---

113. Evidently the true form of the name, attested in both Greek and Latin texts and adopted by Georg Beer in his translation; see Kautzsch, *Apokryphen*, II, 124. The inserted *l* is a characteristic late improvement. In 1:8 the name, still further corrupted, is secondary and to be canceled.

work. Equally erroneous is the ascription to Dorotheus of Tyre, in whose alleged writings it appears. Both Epiphanius and Dorotheus knew Hebrew, and it was natural to think of the one or the other as the possible author or translator of this work. A highly important form of the text is given by the famous Codex Marchalianus of the prophets, known as Q (see Swete's *Introduction,* pp. 144 f.). It is in an introductory section of the manuscript, the work of a slightly later hand (perhaps 7th century).

The Greek of two distinct recensions was printed by Eberhard Nestle in his *Marginalien und Materialien* (Tübingen, 1893), the texts conveniently facing each other on opposite pages. One of the two is from Codex Q, the other is from an old and important Paris manuscript. Theodor Schermann published in the Teubner Series of classics *five* recensions of the Greek, each with its variant readings (Leipzig, 1907).

It is to Nestle, apparently, that recent interest in the Lives is mainly due. He printed in the first edition of his *Syriac Grammar* (1881) a Syriac text abridged from that contained in three manuscripts of the British Museum. An American scholar, Isaac Hall, was moved to translate a longer Syriac version from a manuscript belonging to Union Theological Seminary; also to publish a Greek text of the Q-type from a Philadelphia manuscript; these in 1887 and 1886 respectively. In the second edition of his *Grammar* (1888) Nestle presented an unabridged Syriac text from the three British manuscripts; and a few years later, in the work mentioned above, he contributed a large amount of material both for the literary history and for the criticism of the text. This was made useful in Schermann's far more comprehensive publications in 1907, appearing in the Teubner volume (see above) and in his thorough study of the Lives in *Texte und Untersuchungen, xxxi,* 1–133.

The list of the prophets varies considerably in the different recensions, and so also does the order in which they are arranged. Whether it is possible to determine the original list may be doubted, see however below. The most common order of the "writing prophets" is that which is followed in Swete's *Old Testament in Greek,* the order found in the manuscripts B, Q, and their fellows. There is also a chronological arrangement in which prophets of all classes are included. For present purposes the order adopted in the English Bible seems preferable. The following brief extracts will perhaps suffice to show the nature of these Hebrew legends.

Isaiah. Isaiah of Jerusalem suffered martyrdom under Manasseh, being sawn in two. In his last moments he prayed for water, and the water of Siloa was "sent" (John 9:7) in answer to his prayer. Formerly, at a time when the city was besieged, his prayers had effected that the water of the Virgin's Fountain should come forth intermittently, flowing for the Hebrews but not for the enemy. The memory of the prophet was thus linked up with the water supply of Jerusalem.

The legend locates Isaiah's tomb in a place kept secret, near the royal tombs which David had designed and Solomon had constructed. Mention of these tombs and their treasure suggested the passage 2 Kings 20:12–19, and Hezekiah's folly and its punishment are recounted.

Jeremiah. Jeremiah of Anathoth was buried in Taphnes in Egypt, where the Jews had stoned him to death. He was held in honor by the Egyptians, for he had performed for them a service like that of Saint Patrick in Ireland, driving out the dangerous reptiles from both land and river. Vipers and crocodiles are specified. A tradition handed down by certain men of Egypt (presumably resident in Jerusalem), whose names are given, tells how Alexander the Great transferred the bones of the prophet to Alexandria, whereupon the vipers and crocodiles of that region were put to flight. He (the prophet) also introduced the snake-fighting creatures called *argolai* (see below) to assist in the work.

The rest of the story of Jeremiah is concerned with the legend of the ark of the covenant and the tables of the law, which the prophet concealed in a cave in the mountain near the burial places of Moses and Aaron. This is another form of the legend which is found in Second Maccabees; see §18.

Ezekiel. This prophet also met a violent death at the hands of his own people, being slain in Babylonia by a leader of the Jewish exiles, whom he had rebuked for idol worship. He was buried in the field of Nahor, in the tomb of Shem and Arphaxad the ancestors of Abraham. In a time of famine, when the people were starving, Ezekiel saved their lives by feeding them with fish taken from the Kebar canal. Under the influence of the prophet the fish came in shoals, of their own accord, to be caught. Ezekiel is said to have predicted, concerning this canal, that when it should be full to overflowing the exiles would return to Palestine; when its flow should cease altogether, destruction would come upon all the land. On one occasion, when crowds of the Jews were flocking to the prophet, the Chaldeans suspected an uprising and sent an army to punish the Jews. At Ezekiel's command, the water of the Kebar was held back until the exiles were in safety; when the Chaldeans attempted to follow, they were drowned. The tribes of Dan and Gad, given to idolatry, were Ezekiel's constant enemies, and one of their number was the leader who killed him.

Daniel. Here the chief interest of the popular recital is in the transformation of Nebuchadnezzar; this subject occupies three fourths of the section. The Hebrew imagination had given much attention to the fourth chapter of Daniel. The great king during the time of his punishment was changed into an animal of composite form, having the head and fore parts of a bull, and the legs and hinder parts of a lion. Daniel interpreted this: tyrants in their pleasure-seeking youth are under the yoke of Satan; in their later years they become fierce wild beasts. The king had his lucid intervals when the grass which he ate was digested and became the food of human beings, and at these times he prayed to God. When at last, as the result of Daniel's prayers, he confessed his sin, he was restored to his kingdom.

Amos. Amaziah the priest of Bethel (Am. 7:10–17) continued to be Amos's active enemy, and at last the son of Amaziah killed the prophet with a cudgel.

Obadiah. He is identified with the third captain of fifty (2 Kings 1:13) who was spared by Elijah, after the two former companies with their captains had been destroyed by fire from heaven.

Jonah. His mother, as the legend has it, was the widow of Zarephath in whose house Elijah lodged (1 Kings 17:8–24). The boy Jonah was the one whom the prophet restored to life. His later years were spent in Tyre, among the Gentiles, doing penance, as he said, for his false prophecy against Nineveh. Removing to the Edomite territory, he died there and was buried in the tomb of Othniel the Kenezite, the first of the Judges of Israel.

Habakkuk. Here is given another form of the story told in Bel and the Dragon (see §12). The prophet, a native of Beth-Zachariah, of the tribe of Simeon, prophesied in Jerusalem and foretold the captivity. When the armies of Nebuchadnezzar destroyed the city, he fled to Ostracena in lower Egypt. After returning to his own land, while living a farmer's life, he was accustomed to carry the noonday meal to the reapers of his barley harvest. One day, as the food was delivered to him, he said to his family: I am off for a far country, but will return immediately; if I delay, take the food out to the reapers. As he finished speaking, he was in Babylon handing down Daniel's dinner into the den of lions. Then returning to the farm in Palestine he attended to the meal of the reapers; and he told no one what had happened.

Nathan. It is interesting to find the reprover of David classed as a foreigner, Hebrew only by adoption. According to the legend he was a man of Gibeon, of the Hivites (see Josh. 9:3–27; 11:19), yet a teacher of the law of Moses. He was told, in a revelation, of the sin which his royal pupil was tempted to commit, and set out in haste for Jerusalem, to utter a warning. But Satan ("Beliar") prepared a trap for him. Lying in the road was a dead man stripped naked. The prophet had no choice but to carry the body away and bury it, and before dawn it was revealed to him that in that night David had committed the sin; so he turned back to Gibeon in sorrow.

Aside from the Major and Minor Prophets and Daniel, the Hebrew list appears to have included Nathan, Ahijah the Shilonite (1 Kings 14), Joad [114] (the prophet of 1 Kings 13:1–10), Zechariah the son of Jehoiada (2 Chr. 24:20), and Azariah the son of Oded (2 Chr. 15). These all were familiar in Jewish folklore. There is some reason to believe that the original document contained no other names.

The biographies of Elijah and Elisha do not appear to belong here. Their rather copious material instead of supplementing the Biblical narrative is simply copied out from it, and their Greek text does not seem to be the result of translation. Some ancient manuscripts of the Lives include also Zechariah (Luke 1:5 ff.), Simeon (Luke 2:25 ff.), and John the Baptist. It is moreover to be observed that a distinctly Christian element appears in a number of the principal biographies, the prophet predicting in one form or another the coming of Jesus the Messiah. These Christian passages have been generally recognized, on sufficient grounds, as interpolations.

It has almost always been taken for granted that the Lives in the form known to us must be regarded as an originally Greek composition, even when the existence of a similar work in Hebrew or Aramaic is postulated. The one important exception is the *Commentary* published at Amsterdam in 1833 by the Dutch scholar H. A. Hamaker, who attempted to show in considerable detail that the original language was Hebrew, and the Greek a translation. [115] The attempt failed to carry conviction. Neither Nestle nor Schermann accepted his demonstration as valid, and the latter states his own conclusion on page 122 of the *Texte und Untersuchungen*. In Palestine, he asserts, the Greek idiom was always full of Hebraisms (the delusion cherished by so many scholars!), and consequently the frequent indications of Hebrew pointed out by Hamaker are merely witnesses to the Palestinian origin of the text. Schermann, it should be added, dated the work in the 1st century A.D. and postulated a Hebrew work lying behind it.

The translation-Greek should be obvious to anyone who is familiar with that idiom. The original language was Hebrew, as is shown by

114. Better Jōʿēd; see 2 Chr. 9:29 LXX, comparing the uncertain Hebrew text and Josephus, *Antt.*, 8, viii, 5.

115. I regret to say that I have not been able to get sight of Hamaker's book. It is described in Nestle's *Marginalien*, pp. 5 f.

many clear indications. The proof cannot be set forth here, but it may suffice for the present to offer two curious bits of evidence taken from the story of Jeremiah's dealing with the serpents in Egypt. The Greek εφωθ, "vipers," [116] is the feminine plural of a Hebrew (not Aramaic) word which is obviously the same as the *eph'e*, "viper," of the Old Testament.

The *"argols"* brought in by Jeremiah to fight the serpents have aroused much interest and made no little trouble. The oldest Greek text of the Lives derives these creatures from Argos in Greece, and the learned note is taken over into the lexicon of Suidas (10th century). Only the accidental transposition of a clause in the LXX text (the Latin has the right order) has prevented the commentators from seeing that the ὀφιομάχης, "serpent-fighter," in Lev. 11:22 renders the Hebrew (*h*)*argol* of that verse. Our Greek interpreter of the Hebrew text of the Lives simply transliterated the rare word.[117]

The reason why so little attention has been paid to the *Lives of the Prophets* in recent years is to be found partly in the fact that its Hebrew origin was not known, and partly in the corrupt state of the Greek text, which is in great need of emendation from the Semitic side.

Literature. E. Nestle, *Marginalien und Materialien,* pp. 1–64 (also published separately). Th. Schermann, "Propheten- und Apostellegenden," in *Texte und Untersuchungen,* Bd. *31,* 1–133; also *Prophetarum Vitae* (Leipzig, Teubner, 1907), the Greek and Latin texts. I. H. Hall, *Jour. Bib. Lit., 6* (1886), 27–39 (the Greek text); 7 (1887), 28–39 (translation of a Syriac version). Louis Ginzberg, *Legends of the Jews.*

§36. THE TESTAMENT OF JOB

THIS is another book of the "hidden 70" (2 Esd. 14:46) on which some new light can be thrown. It is older, and more important, than has generally been supposed in modern times. It is a work of a well-known type; Job's parting words to his children continue the literary tradition which was begun in Genesis 49 and Deuteronomy 33 and is rep-

116. The Greek text is badly muddled here, for the inclusion of the crocodiles at this point is plainly a later improvement; so also apparently Schermann, p. 86, decides. In the Syriac version we can even read of healing the "bites" of crocodiles.

117. The "snake-fighter" introduced by Jeremiah is evidently the ichneumon, which in the past has done excellent service in Egypt by killing poisonous serpents and devouring the eggs of crocodiles. The fact appears to be that in Egypt this little animal was popularly called "the grasshopper" because of its marvellously quick leaps. The Greek translator of Lev. 11:22 seems to have been more familiar with this use of the word than with its proper meaning, for in this passage it certainly signifies a variety of locust.

resented in several of the apocryphal books. It has some very interesting features of its own, among them the relation of its Greek text (which is a translation) to the LXX of Job. Since the work is so unfamiliar, it is necessary to give more space than usual to an account of the available literature.

The Greek text was first published by Cardinal Mai, in Vol. VII of his *Scriptorum Veterum Nova Collectio* (Rome, 1833), edited from a single manuscript. A French translation of this was given in Migne's *Dictionnaire des Apocryphes*, II, 403. The work remained unnoticed, however, until the year 1897, when Kaufmann Kohler, in *Semitic Studies in Memory of Dr. Alexander Kohut* (Berlin, 1897), pp. 264–338, reprinted and translated Mai's text with an Introduction and valuable notes.

In the same year, M. R. James, in his *Apocrypha Anecdota*, 2d Ser. (Cambridge, 1897),[118] published a slightly different text from a Paris manuscript of the 11th century, and discussed the work at some length. His introduction occupies pp. lxxii–cii, and on pp. 104–137 he prints the Greek text with the variants of Mai's manuscript at the bottom of the page. In beginning his description of the work he says of it: "Considering its interest, the book has attracted extremely little attention. . . . Speaking broadly, I think we may say that the Testament of Job is practically an unknown book."

The older literary history is not quite a blank. We find the book referred to in the Decree of Gelasius (Bishop of Rome in 492–496), in a long list of apocryphal writings. No. 30 in this list is *Liber qui appellatur 'testamentum Iob' apocryphus*. A question arising much farther back concerns the undoubted connection of the Testament with the Greek translation (the LXX) of the canonical book. Here, as will be seen, one of the two Greek texts borrows verbally from the other, and it has not hitherto been shown which is the original. James left the question undecided, though at one point, the rather long speech of Job's wife in 2:9 of the LXX, he argued acutely (p. lxxix) that the balance of probability favors the Testament as the original. He added: "If that is the case, the Testament must be a very early book."

James never doubted that the book was composed in Greek, and since it contains some phrases plainly reminiscent of the New Testament he was inclined to believe its author a Christian, and therefore its date the 2d or 3d century A.D. How reconcile this with the fact that it is unmistakably a Jewish work? He suggested, as a possible explanation, that its author, a Jew by birth but a Christian in faith, "was putting into Greek a Hebrew Midrash on Job," not translating

118. This constitutes Vol. V of the "Texts and Studies" edited by J. Armitage Robinson.

it but paraphrasing; making much use of the Greek version of Job and using familiar N. T. terms of expression.

Kohler, on the contrary, in the work above mentioned and in his excellent article, "The Testament of Job," *Jewish Encyclopedia*, VII, 200–202, made it plain that the Testament is Jewish through and through, with no evidence of a Christian element. He pointed out numerous Midrashic parallels, and ended his article by saying that "the work is one of the most remarkable productions of the pre-Christian era."

It is indeed a typical midrash, based on the material contained in the canonical Job, but wandering far from it. The imagination of the writer runs riot in all directions, both in inventing details and in creating new scenes, with the homiletic element in the foreground, and the properties and ideas of the author's own day ever present. There is much here to interest the student of the "outside books."

Considering the character of the work, the Greek text has been fairly well preserved. The Paris manuscript, with all its faults, gives unquestionably an older text than the manuscript edited by Mai, from which we get the impression of a version made from memory. But both texts are needed.

Mention was made, above, of a significant relation of some sort existing between the Greek of the Testament and that of the LXX version of Job. The latter has had a peculiar history in more than one respect. In the first place, it is known to be a composite text, an originally much abridged version having been supplemented from the translation of Theodotion.[119] More remarkable is the presence of certain additions to the Greek text corresponding to nothing contained in the Hebrew. One of these additions begins at 2:9, another at 42:17. The latter, which is distinctly midrashic in character, is expressly declared to have been translated from an Aramaic original. As to this, see below. It is the addition which begins at 2:9 that is especially important, for its text is verbally duplicated in the Testament, namely, in chapter 24 and the last paragraph of chapter 25. James presents the two texts in parallel columns, page lxxiv.

The question now arises, whether there is evidence that the Greek of the Testament, in general, gives evidence of borrowing from the LXX of Job. James prints on pages lxxv–lxxix, again in parallel columns, the passages in which there is more or less verbal correspondence, the result showing that there is extremely little agreement of the sort, none in fact that might not be accidental. The conclusion, drawn by James himself, therefore seems practically certain, that this foreign

119. See Swete's *Introduction to the Old Testament in Greek,* pp. 255 ff., and the references given; also Thackeray, *Grammar of the Old Testament in Greek,* pp. 3 f.

element in the LXX text beginning at 2:9 was borrowed from the Testament. It is a reasonable conjecture that the remarkable rearrangement of clauses and sentences was effected in order to conceal the fact of borrowing.

The other addition to the LXX, beginning at 42:17, "translated from the Aramaic book," now takes on new interest, for the Testament, as will presently be shown, was itself originally Aramaic, our Greek being a translation. The material, historical and biographical, here at the end of chapter 42 of the Greek Job would be quite in place as either Introduction or Appendix to the Testament. There may of course have been more than one Aramaic book dealing with the saint and his history, but we have no need to postulate any other. The probability is that both additions in the LXX were taken from one and the same book.

The Greek of the book is very plainly the result of translation from Semitic. Such expressions as Ἰδοὺ ἐγώ, "here am I," 105, 10 (the page numbers of James's edition) ; ἐν τίνι ἐστίν, "in what condition he is," 125, 24 and 126, 3; γαστήρ for "heart" (of affection), 128, 21 ; "inspired by (ἐν) Satan," 130, 20, and a multitude of others, tell a plain story. The Aramaic origin is also evident throughout. Instead of ὁ διάβολος for the Adversary we see everywhere the proper name *Satanā* with the Aramaic definite ending; as in Palestine generally, but not in translations from Hebrew. The word ζῷα for "domestic animals," 114, 2 and 130, 1, renders Aramaic, not Hebrew. "When I *began* to show them," 121, 3 ; "answered and said," 122, 11, 19 (notice the context) ; and finally the Greek τότε, Aram. ʿ*dain*, is incessantly used to carry on the narrative, as so frequently in the pre-Christian Aramaic writings, as well as in the Gospel of Matthew.

An interesting detail which can occasionally be observed is the coincidence of this Aramaic with that of the Targum. In Job 42:10 the saint is rewarded with "double" what he had before. In the corresponding passage in the Testament (chap. 44) the Greek has ἐν τῷ διπλῷ, a strange idiom which is not Hebrew. The Targum in this same place has it exactly, *bᵉkuflā*.

The phrases which might suggest familiarity with the Gospels are merely idioms of the Aramaic popular speech. Σὺ ὄψει, "it is your affair," p. 116, 24, cf. Matt. 27:4, 24. "Be long-suffering toward (ἐπί) us," and we will pay, p. 110, 21, cf. Matt. 18:26, 29. "Unto the end (συντέλεια) of the world," p. 106, 10, as in Matt. 13:39 f., cf. Dan. 12:4, 6, 7, 13. Ὃ ποιεῖς ποίησον, "finish what you are doing," p. 108, 12, cf. John 13:27. Ἀνάστα, ἆρον αὐτήν, "go on and take it!" p. 117, 4, said by Job's wife to the man who was preparing to cut off her hair.

In the Testament, Job's wife Sitidos (on the name, see below) plays a much more important part than in the Hebrew. Though reduced to wretched poverty and near starvation, she supports her husband while he is physically unable to help himself. Harassed by Satan, she at last calls upon Job to curse God and die. Job, as he rebukes her, sees Satan skulking behind her and dares him to come out into the open and fight. He sneaks out and away, discomfited and confessing his inability to cope with the saint. Sitidos lives to see her husband vindicated by God, but not to see him restored to health and affluence. In her last appearance in the story she goes in rags to the three kings, Job's friends, and beseeches them to search the ruins of her house for the remains of her children, so that they may be given burial. Job, hearing this, tells her and the kings that the children are not in the ruins but are in heaven. They declare him insane; but he utters a prayer, and says: "Raise your eyes toward the east!" They look, and see the children wearing heavenly crowns. Sitidos dies on that same day, comforted and in peace. She is mourned throughout the city, and the multitude of the poor to whom she had formerly ministered chant a dirge in memory of her good deeds. This dirge is said to be preserved "in the Chronicles" (cf. 2 Chr. 35:25).

The three friends and Elihu have a prominent part in the narrative, as would be expected. After their attempts to convict Job of sin, they are severely rebuked by the voice of God, threatened with death, and at length pardoned (as in the Hebrew) only through Job's intercession. Elihu comes off much worse than the others. "He is not a man," the divine voice declares to Job, "but a beast ($\theta\eta\rho\text{í}o\nu$)." Eliphaz and his companions take up the accusation, and consign Elihu to Hades, in an antiphonal chant of some length.

After Job's restoration he takes a second wife, Dinah (the name given also in the Targum), who is the mother of the children who gather about him to hear his story and his last words, just before his death. His three daughters are now given an important rôle, as the end comes. Each of the three in turn is inspired, and chants a hymn in the language of the heavenly beings. Job's brother Nahor now takes up the story, telling how at the end of three days they saw shining chariots come to take away the spirit of the saint. The book closes with a brief dirge sung by Nahor, the seven sons, and a throng of those whom Job's bounty had blessed.

The proper names which are peculiar to the Paris text are an amusing collection. The Greek translator, who was also editor, seems to have taken it ill that the names of Job's three daughters should be given while the sons remain anonymous; and even more, that the faithful wife, who stood by Job and suffered with him through all the years of his torture, should not be given a name in the narrative. It is a purely sentimental need that is satisfied, there is no pretense of translation or of ancient authority. The names are neither Greek nor Semitic, and the editor makes it plain that they are inserted to fill a gap.

As for the seven sons, two of them share the name Tersi·choros (evidently Terpsi·choros), which is conveniently divided for the purpose; two others similarly halve Nice·phoros; and to a third pair are assigned the two parts of the name Iphi·phrouron ("mightily guarding").[120] The seventh son is named Ὕων, which is given in Pape-Benseler, *Griechische Eigennamen*, as an Egyptian name. This proceeding of a translator is very instructive.

Equally interesting is the editor's naming of Job's first wife. Here again he would make his own proceeding plain to all readers. Her name is taken from that of Job's own land, she is simply the woman "of Ausitis," (Αὐ)σίτιδος, and throughout the Testament she is given the name Sitidos, later improved in Mai's text to Sitis.

The opinion of Kohler (see above) that the book is pre-Christian seems well founded. This was originally James's view, see page xciii, and he praises the book as a literary production. The Greek translation, an excellent specimen of its kind, also gives the impression of a comparatively early date, and is the work of a scholar of no ordinary equipment and ability. The original work may be assigned to the last century B.C., the translation following it soon.

Literature. The article "Testament of Job" in the *Jewish Encyclopedia*. The Introduction and Greek text published by M. R. James (see above). Kaufmann Kohler's translation (English) in the Alexander Kohut volume, also mentioned above.

120. If the conjecture is permitted. The reading of the manuscript is Phiphi·phrouon, which seems hardly capable of interpretation.

GENERAL INDEX